D1582014

SCOTTISH HISTORY SOCIETY

SIXTH SERIES

VOLUME 12

The Autobiography of Arthur Woodburn
1890–1978

The Autobiography of Arthur Woodburn
1890–1978

Living with History

Edited by
Gordon Pentland

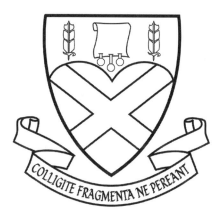

COLLIGITE FRAGMENTA NE PEREANT

SCOTTISH HISTORY SOCIETY
2017

THE BOYDELL PRESS

First published 2017

A Scottish History Society publication
in association with The Boydell Press
an imprint of Boydell & Brewer Ltd
PO Box 9, Woodbridge, Suffolk IP12 3DF, UK

and of Boydell & Brewer Inc.
668 Mt Hope Avenue, Rochester, NY 14620–2731, USA

website: www.boydellandbrewer.com

ISBN 978-0-906245-42-2

A CIP catalogue record for this book is available
from the British Library

The publisher has no responsibility for the continued existence or accuracy of URLs for
external or third-party internet websites referred to in this book, and does not guarantee that
any content on such websites is, or will remain, accurate or appropriate

This publication is printed on acid-free paper

Typeset by HWA Text and Data Management, London, UK

Printed and bound in Great Britain by TJ International Ltd, Padstow, Cornwall

MIX
Paper from
responsible sources
FSC® C013056

CONTENTS

ACKNOWLEDGEMENTS

The current volume could not have been produced without assistance from a number of sources. First and foremost, I gratefully acknowledge the permission of Ken Duffy to use the Woodburn Papers (held at the National Library of Scotland) for this publication. The staff of the Special Collections Reading Room at the National Library of Scotland (in particular, Maria Castrillo, Yvonne Shand and Amy Todman) were unfailingly helpful in contacting copyright holders and in processing a vexatious reprographics order. I am obliged to the School of History, Classics and Archaeology at the University of Edinburgh, which paid for the order. I would like to thank the Scottish History Society for commissioning the volume. In seeing the proposal through to production, John McCallum, the Publications Secretary and General Editor, has been a model of professionalism and good judgment and I extend my thanks to an anonymous reader who made a number of valuable suggestions for improvement of the final text. Finally, I would like to thank Yonsei University in Seoul and DMC Ville 'Serviced Apartments for Foreigners'. Between them they provided a very hospitable environment in which to complete the bulk of the transcription and notes during the summer of 2016 and, along with Arthur Woodburn, they almost succeeded in making me forget how much I missed my family.

Gordon Pentland
7 February 2017

INTRODUCTION

Arthur Woodburn (1890–1978)[1]

It is not entirely surprising that Arthur Woodburn's memoirs were not published during his lifetime. The tone adopted in the different versions of the autobiography – dry, sincere and largely humourless – provides a literary version of his character as recorded by the obituarist for the *Times*:

> … he was representative of many Socialists of an older school. Solid, slow and deliberate in speech, yet not without a definite personal charm, earnest and immensely conscientious, he took all his duties with great seriousness but lacked the depth and suppleness of intellect to make a substantial impression on his times[2]

When set alongside the full-bodied and combative memoirs by contemporaries such as David Kirkwood or Willie Gallacher, or the witty and more self-consciously literary effort by his close colleague and predecessor as Secretary of State for Scotland, Tom Johnston, Woodburn's inevitably suffer by the comparison.[3] This volume, therefore, requires some justification.

---

[1] There are useful biographical sketches of Arthur Woodburn [hereafter AW] in W. W. Knox, 'Woodburn, Arthur (1890–1978)', in W. W. Knox (ed.), *Scottish Labour Leaders 1918–39: A Biographical Dictionary* (Edinburgh, 1984), 284–9; C. Harvie, 'Woodburn, Arthur (1890–1978)', *Oxford Dictionary of National Biography*, Oxford University Press, 2004, online edn, January 2008[http://www.oxforddnb.com/view/article/56498, accessed 8 September 2016].

[2] 'Mr Arthur Woodburn: Former Secretary of State for Scotland', *Times*, 3 June 1978.

[3] D. Kirkwood, *My Life of Revolt* (London, 1935); W. Gallacher, *Revolt on the Clyde: An Autobiography* (London, 1936); W. Gallacher, *The Last Memoirs of William Gallacher* (London, 1966); T. Johnston, *Memories* (London, 1952).

The active years of Woodburn's life coincided with the formation and 'rise' of the Labour Party. Woodburn's memoirs follow the standard syntax of political autobiography. An account of Woodburn's political formation and childhood memories prefaces in-depth recollections of involvement in or attitudes towards transformative political moments: the First World War, the tribulations of two minority Labour governments and the internecine disputes within the interwar movement, and the experience of coalition government after 1940. The terminus reached is the achievements of the Labour governments of 1945 to 1951. By 1948 the ideals of socialist pioneers had become 'accepted as national policy' and a 'peaceful social revolution' had been achieved.[4] Pen portraits and evaluations of friends, acquaintances, colleagues and antagonists pepper the text along with anecdotes derived from childhood, work and Parliament.

The perspective from which Woodburn narrated the twentieth-century history of the Labour movement is an interesting and underrepresented one. To begin with, it is worth noting that the narrative is an Edinburgh-centred one. Additionally, the institutional anchors for Woodburn's career were the Labour College movement and the Labour Party rather than the trades unions or, for much of his career, the Independent Labour Party (ILP). Woodburn was a union member – of the National Union of Clerks – but he was so as someone with a management position in his firm. His experiences were not, therefore, ones that feature very prominently within existing published sources on the Labour movement, which tend to speak with a Glaswegian accent (or at least recount Glasgow-based experiences) or else relate political developments from a trades union perspective.

A second justification is that Woodburn did not style himself as a 'troublemaker'. These are not the memoirs of an outsider. They instead present the *Weltanschauung* of a consummate Labour loyalist. There is a sense, of course, in which Woodburn was burnishing past militancy in respectable old age. He did spend years in prison for his opposition to conscription and his retelling of these experiences is especially rich in detail. As an ILP member from 1916, Woodburn voted for the party to join the Third (Communist) International after the First World War. The more plausible explanation, however, is that he simply was not one of life's rebels and that following these youthful experiences, he settled down from his thirties to become a model of Labour probity and common sense. He is a mouthpiece for a post-war Scottish Labour mentality of responsible economic planning and moderate politics. The pose adopted most frequently is that of the reluctant manager, not

---

4   See below, pp. 3, 143.

especially thirsty for executive office, but willing and ready to deploy his skills at the behest and in the service of the wider movement. The main roles that he played – within the National Council of Labour Colleges (NCLC), as organiser and secretary for the Labour Party in Scotland, as Secretary of State for Scotland – are all presented in that way. There is a thinly disguised contempt throughout for flashier politicians accompanied by a formulaic preference for the 'doer' over the 'speaker'.

It is principally the uniqueness of the angle which justifies the publication of the text that follows. While it covers events that can be found elsewhere – no-conscription activism, the General Strike, Labour's battle with the left in the 1930s, nationalism in the 1940s – it does so from an uncommon perspective. That generation of Scottish Labour MPs who carried the party into its post-war triumph has a spokesperson in Arthur Woodburn. Fundamentally, these are the memoirs of an effective and earnest Labour bureaucrat.

The Making of a Socialist

Woodburn hailed from Edinburgh's 'labour aristocracy', that upper stratum of the working class which came to share a distinctive identity and to espouse a particular matrix of social values from the middle of the nineteenth century. His father's brass foundry business may well have served as a playground and to acquaint Woodburn with the 'language of the workshop', but his own trajectory took him through Bruntsfield and Boroughmuir schools into clerical work. This migration of men from skilled working families into clerical or business occupations was relatively common, 'a move within the artisan social world, rather than … a foothold on the lower reaches of the bourgeois world'.[5] Nonetheless, the family ethic of self-improvement could also be presented as an aspiration for social mobility. Woodburn recounts his eldest brother's ultimately successful argument against him becoming an engineer's apprentice: 'no one got anywhere in modern society who took his coat off to work'.[6] By his own account, Woodburn's love of learning came reasonably late in his schooling (he left school at the age of fourteen in 1904), but thereafter it was a constant. He attended Heriot-Watt College (then based on Chambers Street in Edinburgh) four or five nights a week, learning languages and commercial and accounting subjects and latterly turned his attention to economics.

---

[5]   R. Q. Gray, *The Labour Aristocracy in Victorian Edinburgh* (Oxford, 1976), 135.
[6]   See below, p. 11.

The formation of Woodburn's politics seems to have taken a well-trodden route from an instinctive Liberal radicalism, through the crucible of the constitutional crisis around the People's Budget and the First World War, to an ethical socialism realised through the ILP. The church and an evangelical religion lies in the background, as it did for so much of Labour's personnel and outlook in Scotland and beyond.[7] Work experience from 1904 in a legal firm representing the 'Wee Frees' in their celebrated controversy with the United Free Church had a marked impact. It exposed Woodburn to a combative species of politics, whose similarities with the fissile Labour politics of the interwar years allowed him to draw ready comparisons. It also cured him of any very high regard for organised religion, while leaving behind the essentially religious and evangelical sensibility and outlook of the ethical socialist.

Liberalism was the family inheritance and Woodburn recalls reading the newspaper to his father (who died when Woodburn was nine) and listening intently to political discussions around the Boer War. He even somewhat hazily recounts involvement on the Liberal side at a hotly-contested Edinburgh by-election in 1899. In the main, however, his politicisation occurred after school. One site was the debating club of Heriot-Watt College, one node in that dense network of university and civic associations in Britain, which reproduced ideas of good citizenship and trained diverse groups in the practice of public speaking.[8] He took the Liberal side in the prolonged disputes around the People's Budget, but by his own admission, Woodburn was 'more a listener than speaker'.[9] One influence there and beyond was William Young Darling (1885–1962), whose political journey from a youthful socialism to Unionism is recounted in Woodburn's autobiography.

The more intellectualised account of his political development namechecks seminal texts within the wider labour movement. The political economy of the nineteenth-century critic John Ruskin, which Woodburn cites in his own development, was, with the work of Thomas Carlyle, the most frequently mentioned text in a revealing 1906 survey of Labour notables and those books that had influenced them.[10] The more contemporary works Woodburn mentions as formative – Norman Angell's *The Great Illusion* (1910) and Henry

[7] W. W. Knox, 'Religion and the Scottish Labour Movement, c. 1900–1939', *Journal of Contemporary History*, xxiii (1988), 609–30.
[8] J. S. Meisel, *Public Speech and the Culture of Public Life in the Age of Gladstone* (New York, 2001), ch. 1.
[9] See below, p. 15.
[10] M. Bevir, *The Making of British Socialism* (Princeton, 2011), 235.

Brailsford's *The War of Steel and Gold* (1914) – were best sellers and helped to shape a generation of Labour politicians and activists.[11]

If those influences were general, a more specific one was found in the genial company of William Graham (1887–1932), a near contemporary of Woodburn's, who fired his enthusiasm for economics through his lectures at Heriot-Watt College. Indeed, it is not too fanciful to draw parallels between their two lives. Graham's ascent was faster and higher – he became Financial Secretary to the Treasury and key ally of Labour Chancellor Philip Snowden in 1924, then President of the Board of Trade in 1929–31 – but their backgrounds, interests and experiences were similar. Before the First World War, Graham was an exemplar of the kind of restless political, social and educational activism that would mark Woodburn's own development.[12] Other unnamed influences were also important, including the almost stock character of the socialist railwayman – named in one version of the autobiography as William Proudfoot – who propagandised Woodburn on his way to work at the London Road foundry of Robert Miller.[13]

Involvement in the opposition to conscription and his imprisonment, however, were clearly the transformative events in Woodburn's early life. The First World War thus completed his politicisation and he joined both the No-Conscription Fellowship and the ILP in 1916. This opposition was doubtless in part inspired by his reading of Brailsford and Angell, but it was also rooted in the experience of the small firm for which he worked, which confronted the monopoly practices of the big armaments firms from 1914. Woodburn was just one of many who either found in opposition to conscription an outlet for their already-existing socialism, or whose socialism was confirmed or developed by such activism.[14]

Arrested and court-martialled for the first time in November 1916, Woodburn was court-martialled another four times and was not released until summer 1919. As someone in a reserved occupation, Woodburn deliberately sought confrontation, giving full rein to his 'hair-splitting conscience' by writing to the authorities to declare his opposition both to conscription and to the war, and appealing each

[11] See, for example, the reference to Brailsford in the political formation of Emrys Hughes in Knox (ed.), *Scottish Labour Leaders*, 144.
[12] T. N. Graham, *Willie Graham: The Life of the Rt. Hon. W. Graham* (London, 1948).
[13] See, for example, the role of a socialist signalman on the Edinburgh–Peebles line on J. P. M. Millar, J. McIlroy, 'Obituary: J. P. M. Millar (1893–1989)', *Labour History Review*, lv (1990), 4–6.
[14] W. Kenefick, 'War Resisters and Anti-conscription in Scotland: An ILP Perspective', in C. M. M. Macdonald and E. W. McFarland (eds), *Scotland and the Great War* (Edinburgh, 1999), 59–80.

tribunal decision.[15] He explained his reasons in the kind of language beloved by war resisters and indicated the recent provenance of his socialist critique of the war:

> I am conscientiously opposed to taking human life, and to taking part in war. I also object on principle to the Government or any section of the people attempting to force me into such military service. I may state that although I have domestic reasons enough – which I do not wish to discuss – to warrant my declining service, I state my appeal solely on conscientious grounds, believing as I do in the vital principle involved.
>
> I understand from the newspapers that the Local Tribunal was influenced by the length of time these convictions have been held, but although I could not honestly claim long standing, I can only solemnly affirm that they are strong, and that nothing will make me depart from them. I am a socialist and believe that a collectivist state would solve all wars. I believe that the fact of my being a badged man, also influenced the decision, but as I stated I could not be expected to leave my regular work but I do not wish this to be made a condition of exemption.[16]

Woodburn's accounts of the petty humiliations and small consolations involved in the experience and of the friends and acquaintances met during his tour of Glencorse Barracks, Wormwood Scrubs, the Tower of London and, in particular, Calton Jail, is the most lively and richly detailed part of the autobiography. It adds detail and a different perspective to similar narratives in, for example, Gallacher's memoirs.[17]

As it always has for radicals, imprisonment both expanded Woodburn's network (he was imprisoned alongside James Maxton, James MacDougall, Bob Stewart and Willie Gallacher) and allowed him to further his education. Prolonged solitary confinement was eased by religious texts, classic self-help literature and re-engagement with Scott's novels. More important for his political development was that a humane chaplain at Calton allowed for access to Marx's *Capital*, on the grounds that he himself had looked through it while studying economics at university and could find nothing about socialism. His

[15] National Library of Scotland [hereafter: NLS], Woodburn Papers, Acc. 7656 [hereafter: Woodburn Papers], Box 2/1, Robert E. Miller to AW, 21 November 1917.
[16] National Records of Scotland, Military Service Tribunals, HH 30/2/1/14, Notice of Appeal, 20 March 1916.
[17] Gallacher, *Revolt on the Clyde*, ch. 7.

engagement with the Marxist canon was evident in much of his later writing.

The prison years were important ones for Woodburn's political development, but they were also crucial in a personal sense. Woodburn was now absolutely committed to the Labour movement and, on his release, he married within the movement. Woodburn met Barbara Halliday, a teacher from an ILP-supporting family, through his involvement in the recreational side of socialist politics. She remained very active within the Labour movement and contested Edinburgh South in the 1935 general election and sat, from 1937, as a Labour councillor in Edinburgh. It was clearly a strong relationship and Woodburn nearly always discussed important career and political decisions with his wife.

These were thus important formative years. Of all of the autobiographical sketches in his papers, it was his experience during the First World War which he returned to most frequently and reworked. It had forged his most important personal relationship, crystallised his political commitments and bequeathed him some cachet within a Labour movement which tended to valorise imprisoned martyrs. In 1931, when Calton Jail was being demolished to make way for the construction of St Andrew's House, Woodburn made a point of buying stones from the site. He used them to pave his garden on Orchard Road in Edinburgh, a fact about him that was frequently repeated by journalists.[18]

Educator and Journalist

Returning to work at Miller's, Woodburn expanded his professional horizons by taking charge of the development of new costing systems. He also threw himself into the field of workers' education and began to lecture in economics for the Edinburgh district of the Scottish Labour College, commuting to the mining towns around Edinburgh to lecture on finance, economics and history. This commitment was driven by two influential people in Woodburn's life. First, John S. Clarke (1885–1959), who had moved to Edinburgh in 1910. Clarke was a charismatic lecturer and member of the Socialist Labour Party, whose lectures, illuminated by lantern-slides, attracted large audiences before and after the war.[19] The Woodburns were frequent visitors to

[18] NLS, Woodburn Papers, Box 2/1, [untitled newspaper clipping] 3 February 1931; 'A Teacher Takes Over', *Daily Mail*, 8 October 1947; 'Mr Woodburn has Souvenir of Jail Days', *Aberdeen Press and Journal*, 8 October 1947.
[19] W. Kenefick, *Red Scotland! The Rise and Fall of the Radical Left, c. 1872 to 1932* (Edin-

his Morningside home and Woodburn's rapidly growing commitment to the Scottish Labour College mirrored Clarke's own enhanced involvement into the 1920s.

The second, J. P. M. Millar (1893–1989), was, like Woodburn, from an essentially clerical background and had engaged before the war with two key institutions of workers' education, the Plebs League and the Central Labour College in London. During the war, he was the Edinburgh branch organiser for the No-Conscription Fellowship. Millar was a prominent figure within the Scottish Labour College and, as staff tutor for the Edinburgh district following the war, began a life-long collaboration with Woodburn, to whom he was temperamentally matched. It was his preferred model for part-time day and weekend classes over John Maclean's aspirations for a full-time residential workers' college that drove the latter from the Scottish Labour College. When a co-ordinating body – the NCLC – was founded in 1921, the Edinburgh district was in rude health (accounting for 27 classes and 917 students of the Scottish Labour College's 65 and 2200). Millar took over as secretary of the NCLC in 1923 and ran it from his Elm Row house until its functions were taken over by the Trades Union Congress (TUC) in 1963. Woodburn became ever more heavily involved in the NCLC, acting as secretary for the Edinburgh district of the Scottish Labour College and eventually becoming president of the NCLC in 1937.[20]

With a teacher as a wife and his own experience of learning and teaching, it is easy to see how education became central to Woodburn's vision of how society would transition to socialism. It is notable that his commitment was to the Labour College movement, whose espousal of 'independence' in working-class education was in part a repudiation of the models provided by Ruskin College and the Workers' Educational Association.[21] His own publications radiated that more general suspicion of the educational framework provided by existing institutions.[22] It was one aspect of his career about which Woodburn felt extremely passionate. When offered the role of secretary

burgh, 2007), 167. For Clarke's career, see R. Challinor, *John S. Clarke: Parliamentarian, Poet and Lion-tamer* (London, 1977). AW corresponded extensively with Challinor over the biography, NLS, Woodburn Papers Box 1/3.

[20] J. P. M. Millar, *The Labour College Movement* (London, 1976).

[21] On the politics of adult education in this period, see J. Rose, *The Intellectual Life of the British Working Classes* (New Haven and London), chs 8–9; S. Macintyre, *A Proletarian Science: Marxism in Britain, 1917–1933* (London, 1986).

[22] 'Scottish School Books', *Scotsman*, 13 June 1934; J. P. M. Millar and AW, *Bias in the Schools* (London, 1936); AW, *Education and the Struggle for Power* (London, 1937).

and organiser for the Labour Party in Scotland, his one caveat was that he be permitted to continue his educational work.[23]

Such activities gave focus and shape to Woodburn's thinking: he was not the first or the last to discover that writing a course of lectures on a subject enforces a steep learning curve on the lecturer. During the period of the General Strike and the internecine and partisan disputes that surrounded the collapse of the Labour government of 1929 to 1931, Woodburn (along with figures like Charles Gibbons) developed workers' education around Edinburgh in the direction set by Millar: less an autonomous and revolutionary seedbed and more a centralised and efficient, but crucially independent, educational service for trades unions. Through his educational activities, Woodburn was increasingly identified with the mainstream of the Labour movement, against both communist efforts at subversion and the insurgent left-wing of the ILP.

The NCLC was an important outlet for these efforts and it was in preparing a course of lectures on finance in 1928 that Woodburn began to contemplate the practical financial issues that would face an incoming Labour government. A widely delivered lecture on 'The Problems of a Future Labour Government', educational and polemical pamphlets (most notably *The Banks and the Workers* and *The Mystery of Money*) and a more substantial textbook, *An Outline of Finance*, lent him greater influence within the movement.[24] His more popular works went into numerous editions and both the *Mystery of Money* and the *Outline of Finance* were still being printed after the Second World War. Woodburn took great satisfaction in the circulation and supposed impact of these educational works. For example, he recounts that a group of West Lothian miners, who had attended his lecture, later rejected the left-wing Cook-Maxton manifesto of 1928 as utopian on the basis of his teaching. These works even afforded him some glimmer of an international reputation, and the Australian Labour Prime Minister, John Curtin, visiting the UK during the Second World War, highlighted his familiarity with Woodburn's *Outline*.

The serious study of economics, begun before the war, helped Woodburn arrive at the sorts of gradualist approach that would mark his politics in the 1920s and 1930s. Like many of those who engaged with Marx's works from the 1880s onwards, Woodburn seems to have read *Capital* as a work whose most important demonstration was the inevitability of the demise of capitalism. It was a recurrent theme not

---

[23] NLS, Woodburn Papers, Box 2/6, AW to Ben Shaw, 8 June 1932.
[24] AW, *The Banks and the Workers* (London, 1925); AW, *The Mystery of Money or the Uses and Abuses of the Banks* (London, 1929); AW, *An Outline of Finance* (London, 1930).

only in the educational texts he produced, but also in his voluminous journalism of the interwar period. From the late 1920s he became a prolific contributor to the socialist press, appearing regularly in the *Forward* and *Plebs*. One example, from the Edinburgh newspaper of which he acted as editor, the *Labour Standard*, gives an insight into his essentially didactic style and his deployment of Marx:

> Socialism will be the heir to capitalism. Capitalism from the development of its inherent forces will create such internal and external difficulties that war or revolution will certainly overtake it, and the greater the ruin, the greater would be the difficulties in the creation of Socialism. We can say, like our comrade, that we will confine ourselves to preparing the worker mentally for the new society, and point to the increasing misery as illustrations of our theories, the complete ruin of unassisted capitalism being handed to Labour when it is past repair, or we can, by taking advantage of every breakdown of capitalism, endeavour to introduce institutions which are making towards Socialism, and by practical demonstration, as well as by theoretical exposition, prove that capitalism cannot meet the needs of society, and that only the complete Socialisation of the means of production and distribution will make a human brotherhood possible.[25]

Knox very aptly sees in Woodburn's reading of Marx and his subsequent career the emergence of a kind of Fabian mentality, as Woodburn became ever more interested in how the state might plan for a peaceful and harmonious transition from capitalism to socialism.[26] We should not overstate the speed of Woodburn's adoption of these positions. In a short passage in the autobiography, for example, he bluntly reveals that he voted with the 'left' wing of the ILP for affiliation to the Third (Communist) International after the First World War. Both his initial reading of Marx and his dispiriting experience of the General Strike, however, helped to underline his essentially gradualist approach.

Woodburn's profile within the Labour movement was thus augmented during the 1920s and this helps to explain his adoption as a Labour candidate for South Edinburgh in 1929. He offered evidence on behalf of the NCLC to the Macmillan committee (set up by Philip Snowden in the aftermath of the Wall Street Crash) and, even if we take his claims to have influenced Keynes's response to the crisis with a

---

[25] 'Reform or Revolution?', *Labour Standard*, 10 Dec. 1927.
[26] Knox, 'Woodburn', 285–6.

large pinch of salt, Woodburn had very clearly emerged as a substantial voice within the Labour movement.[27]

Organiser and MP

This range of experience and clear evidence of administrative efficiency equipped Woodburn well for available parliamentary contests, but even more for organisational roles. He was sounded out in June 1932 by the soon-to-retire Scottish district organiser and Scottish secretary of the Labour Party, Ben Shaw, about whether he might consider succeeding him to the post.[28] It is revealing of Woodburn's nature that he was content to follow the party's line on this appointment, even though it entailed a moratorium on his parliamentary aspirations, an immediate reduction in his salary and the prospect of a further five per cent reduction as a cost-cutting measure. His service ethic won out and in any case, he resignedly commented, he and his wife had 'already allowed themselves to become absorbed by the Movement'.[29]

Following a visit to the Soviet Union with his wife, which confirmed his faith in orderly economic planning, he returned to discover that the appointment had not been as straightforward as Shaw and others had indicated.[30] A candidate had been proposed by the Scottish executive and the national executive had to override its suggestion. The challenges facing Woodburn as secretary were substantial indeed. As a man of wide acquaintance and organisational ability, with the added benefit of access to the press, Woodburn was in a good position to meet them head on: 'I knew the ILP, the CP [Communist Party] and all the other P's which were preventing a united Labour Party'.[31]

The first and immediately most disruptive challenge came with the disaffiliation of the ILP, under the leadership of James Maxton, from the Labour Party in 1932. In the Scottish environment and around Glasgow in particular, where the ILP was the most vibrant wing of the Labour Party, the effect was potentially catastrophic.[32] The presence of more ideologically obnoxious challengers in Glasgow, most notably the Scottish Protestant League, contributed to an uneasy *modus vivendi*

---

[27] NLS, Woodburn Papers, Box 10/5, AW's evidence to the Macmillan Committee, 'Banking Currency and Credit in Relation to Industry and Unemployment', 1930.
[28] NLS, Woodburn Papers, Box 2/6, Ben Shaw to AW, 7 June 1932.
[29] NLS, Woodburn Papers, Box 2/6, AW to Ben Shaw, 8 June 1932.
[30] NLS, Woodburn Papers, Box 2/5, 'Notes regarding Visit to Russia – 16 July to 2 Aug. 1932'.
[31] See below, p. 73.
[32] A. McKinlay and R. J. Morris (eds), *The ILP on Clydeside, 1893–1932: From Foundation to Disintegration* (Manchester, 1991).

and in 1933, the combined efforts of Labour and the ILP (though they contested nine seats with one another) took control of the corporation from the Moderates.[33] Nonetheless, as Maxton and the ILP abandoned gradualism and pilloried its defenders, conflict was intermittent and was especially bitter during the 1935 general election. It was in the context of these struggles that Woodburn developed his unflattering opinions on Maxton as a magnetic but fundamentally irresponsible politician: the 'prophet' to Woodburn's 'practical statesman'. During the 1930s, he came into conflict with most of the 'Clydesiders' who had remained with the ILP and carried forward an image of them that appears frequently in the autobiography, as it did in his review of Keith Middlemas's seminal history: 'The Clydesiders were romantic revolutionaries and prophets and they left it to others to do the day-to-day work of solving the problems.'[34]

As the man in charge of the 'day-to-day' work, ILP disaffiliation generated an additional challenge for Woodburn around the role and nature of the Scottish Socialist Party (SSP), established by ILP members who wished to maintain their affiliation to the Labour Party. Though driven together by their common goals (opposition to communist input and to ILP independence), the SSP and the Labour Party did not always coexist peacefully. Not least, the SSP's efforts to keep the Labour Party at arm's length and so retain the kind of autonomy and nimbleness enjoyed for so long by the ILP, as well as the prominent public profile enjoyed by its leading figure, Pat Dollan, created problems for Woodburn. Running through his criticisms of both the ILP and the SSP is a conventional critique of political irresponsibility, the bureaucrat's disdain for colourful and spontaneous interventions when contrasted with the task of mobilising his own sluggish party machinery.

The final challenge was the relationship between the Labour Party and the Communist Party of Great Britain (CPGB) within the rapidly shifting international context. Such challenges absorbed increasing amounts of Woodburn's time in the second half of the 1930s and he maintained a large file of papers, notes and clippings on Communist Party activities.[35] In the context of the 'popular front' policy of the Communist International after 1935 (which instructed communist parties to embrace parts of the 'progressive bourgeoisie' in the fight against fascism), Woodburn was responsible

---

[33] J. J. Smyth, *Labour in Glasgow, 1896–1936: Socialism, Suffrage, Sectarianism* (Edinburgh, 2000), ch. 6.
[34] 'Review of *The Clydesiders*', *Scotsman*, 27 November 1965; K. Middlemas, *The Clydesiders: A Left Wing Struggle for Parliamentary Power* (London, 1965).
[35] NLS, Woodburn Papers, Box 9.

for disciplining constituency parties and ensuring that delegates and candidates supported Labour Party policy.[36] Woodburn also took part as a polemicist, most notably through the columns of the *Forward*, where his didactic style, honed as a lecturer, was used to good effect, especially in quoting Marx and Lenin back at communists and their sympathisers.[37]

Judged by the scale of these challenges, Woodburn's tenure as secretary was a qualified success. Though the party did not recover all of the ground lost in 1931, Labour's Scottish performance in 1935 was a dramatic improvement. By the end of the decade, the ILP had been effectively sidelined, one of its MPs had rejoined the Labour Party and the SSP had been absorbed. Admittedly, Woodburn was the beneficiary of fair winds as much as the generator of his own successes. In spite of these achievements, going into the Second World War Scottish Labour Party membership remained the lowest of all British regions and constituency Labour parties in Scotland were patchy and frequently dysfunctional.

In view of the acuteness of the crisis of ILP disaffiliation in Scotland and the need 'practically to build from scratch', Woodburn's achievement was substantial.[38] Arguably, the shape of the Labour Party's recovery in Scotland came at a cost. In navigating the post-ILP period, Woodburn had been instrumental in the move towards centralisation entailed in both combating the ILP and communists and in supporting greater levels of planning in the economy. If Woodburn can claim considerable credit for rehabilitating Labour's fortunes north of the border, he was also a key protagonist in turning it 'from a crusade into a machine'.[39]

[36] B. Pimlott, *Labour and the Left in the 1930s* (Cambridge, 1977), ch. 15. See, for example, AW's interventions at the annual conference of the Scottish council of the Labour Party, 'No Popular Front: Scottish Labour Party's Conference', *Scotsman*, 28 May 1938.

[37] See, for example, 'Open Letter to Stalin', *Forward*, 20 November 1937; 'Communists as a Hindrance to Unity: A Final Reply to J. R. Campbell', *Forward*, 8 January 1938. AW's *Forward* articles during this period are collected in Woodburn Papers, Box 24/2.

[38] See, especiallbecame move recognisablehat his image istic activities certainly served to raise his own profile within the movement. Communisty, C. Harvie, 'Labour in Scotland during the Second World War', *Historical Journal*, xxvi (1983), 921–44; W. W. Knox and A. McKinlay, 'The re-making of Scottish Labour in the 1930s', *Twentieth Century British History*, vi (1995), 174–93; I. S. Wood, 'Hope Deferred: Labour in Scotland in the 1920s' and I. Donnachie, 'Scottish Labour in Depression: The 1930s', in I. Donnachie, C. Harvie and I. S. Wood (eds), *Forward! Labour Politics in Scotland 1888–1988* (Edinburgh, 1989), 30–65.

[39] B. McLean, 'Labour in Scotland since 1945: Myth and Reality', in G. Hassan (ed.), *The Scottish Labour Party: History, Institutions and Ideas* (Edinburgh, 2004), 34.

His stint as secretary and his journalistic activities certainly served to raise his own profile within the movement. Woodburn came to be identified as a mouthpiece for Labour policy in Scotland and a benchmark of party orthodoxy. One measure of this is that his image became more recognisable, not least through the Frank Horrabin profile sketch of Woodburn, hand in pocket and sporting a box-tie, which accompanied his *Forward* articles. It also greatly assisted his chances of becoming an MP.

Before his appointment as secretary, Woodburn had been taking steps towards a parliamentary career, having unsuccessfully contested elections in 1929 (Edinburgh South) and 1931 (Leith). The appointment as secretary had, however, lent him much greater experience as an electoral organiser and he effectively acted as agent at a number of by-elections. When Lauchlan Weir died in 1939, Woodburn was selected from five nominees to contest his seat of East Stirling and Clackmannanshire. Doing so in the very opening stages of the Second World War, he was one of the first to benefit from the electoral truce between parliamentary parties, having to face only a pacifist candidate, Andrew Stewart, the assistant editor of *Peace News*. In a low turnout, Woodburn achieved a straightforward victory. It was the seat he would hold (with small boundary revisions in 1950) until his retirement in 1970.

In Parliament Woodburn's competencies fitted him for special, albeit not very glamorous, roles and he set about the task of becoming a useful, active and efficient backbencher and committee man. As someone with a command of details and an interest in administrative process, he was an active member of the Select Committee on National Expenditure and then pursued and chaired a sub-committee on Finance and Establishments. Throughout this parliamentary work, Woodburn drew upon practical experience in costings and organisation and his own intellectual interests in finance.

Woodburn's first important role, the one that marked him as a candidate for future ministerial office, was as Parliamentary Private Secretary to Tom Johnston, Secretary of State for Scotland in Churchill's wartime coalition. In that role, Woodburn became involved in the myriad responsibilities of the Scottish Office and was exposed to Johnston's well-publicised efforts to craft a distinctly Scottish consensus during the war, notably through his council of ex-Secretaries of State.[40] Even before his appointment, Woodburn had

---

[40] G. Walker, *Thomas Johnston* (Manchester, 1988), ch. 6; C. Harvie, 'Labour and Scottish Government: The Age of Tom Johnston', *Bulletin of Scottish Politics*, ii (1981), 1–20.

been exploring wartime expedients of a similar nature and wrote to Churchill in October 1940 recommending the establishment of a grand consultative council of Scottish MPs to sit in Edinburgh.[41]

The role he clearly coveted after Labour's 1945 victory was as Financial Secretary to the Treasury (a post which went to William Glenvil Hall). Woodburn was instead given a junior ministerial role within the Ministry of Supply and Aircraft Production, where again his engineering and managerial background were thought of as an asset. He was allowed considerable autonomy over particular areas of policy (aluminium house production and civilian aircraft) while the ministry of which he was a part navigated the vexed and controversial issue of iron and steel nationalisation.

Scottish Secretary

When Woodburn's minister, John Wilmot, was dismissed in October 1947, so too was Joseph Westwood, who had enjoyed a singularly unhappy tenure as Secretary of State for Scotland since 1945. Westwood had struggled to make the transition from junior minister to a position that entailed a much greater public role as well as the wider responsibilities of cabinet membership.[42] Woodburn had a similarly tempestuous tenure of the post.

The issues faced by the Secretary of State for Scotland were partly structural. As well as playing a role in cabinet, he or she had responsibility for all of the (ever increasing) functions fulfilled by the Scottish Office. Westwood had repeated a characterisation of the post, which had become common currency from the 1920s, as being equivalent to being 'the Pooh-Bah for Scotland'.[43] Such a wide remit was also exacerbated by the peculiar scale of the challenges after 1945, the additional problems after the 'financial Dunkirk' of 1947 and the associated shortages of goods and materials, and the level of ambition embodied by the post-war Labour governments.[44] Finally, the role was a much more public one, with a Secretary of State guaranteed to be covered in the Scottish press and expected to host press conferences at St Andrew's House.[45]

---

[41] NLS, Woodburn Papers, Box 1/1, Winston Churchill to AW, 25 November 1940.
[42] G. Pottinger, *The Secretaries of State for Scotland 1926–76: Fifty Years of the Scottish Office* (Edinburgh, 1979), ch. 10.
[43] J. Mitchell, *Governing Scotland: The Invention of Administrative Devolution* (Basingstoke, 2003), ch. 9.
[44] K. O. Morgan, *Labour in Power 1945–51* (Oxford, 1984).
[45] I. MacDougall, *Voices of Scottish Journalists: Recollections by 22 Veteran Scottish Journalists*

Woodburn inherited the two key challenges that had bewildered Westwood: housing and nationalism. In his autobiography Woodburn explains his limited successes around the first challenge with a slightly grumpy dismissal of the sort of quantitative arguments at play as housing became a key indicator of government success in reconstruction. In short, Woodburn believed that housing was not the main priority, which lay in more general economic reconstruction. He was not helped by one of his undersecretaries, John Robertson, playing the numbers game and making overly optimistic forecasts in public.[46]

Woodburn did improve on Westwood's performance, partly by ensuring a focus on the completion of houses rather than the beginning of new ones. He also pushed through policies to provide for housing to address the relatively higher rates of tuberculosis in Scotland. The context, however, became ever more challenging. The dollar crisis and devaluation necessarily impacted on public expenditure for housing, while Woodburn's partisan preference against the private building of houses was necessarily held against him as slowing down the overall volume of building.[47]

Nationalism was the stickier problem and it was the one that confronted Woodburn most immediately and acutely on his accession to office. He was faced with that common twentieth-century challenge identified by Iain McLean: 'Scottish Labour politicians have had to resolve the tensions between their Scottishness and their Labourness.'[48] At root this was a dilemma with longer provenance, but which crystallised in the particular post-war context: how was it possible to reconcile an instinctive preference for distinctively Scottish control of economic and social life with wider aspirations to nationalise and therefore centralise?

The context driving action on the question was the vociferous presence and activities of the Scottish Convention and, latterly, the Covenant movement. The Convention was the vehicle of the veteran home ruler John MacCormick, who had left the Scottish National Party (SNP) in 1942. It represented a rehabilitation of the strategies of the old Scottish Home Rule Association: the attempt to create a cross-party consensus in favour of home rule and to use that to

---

of their Life and Work (Edinburgh, 2013), 136. For the role of and challenges to the Scottish Office more generally, see I. Levitt (ed.), *The Scottish Office: Depression and Reconstruction 1919–59* (Edinburgh, 1992).

[46] 'Housing Speedup Required: Mr J. J. Robertson's Warning', *Scotsman*, 22 September 1949.

[47] Levitt (ed.), *Scottish Office*, 292–303.

[48] I. McLean, 'Scottish Labour and British Politics', in Hassan (ed.), *Scottish Labour Party*, 148.

extract concessions from the governing party.[49] It found fertile soil in the colourless post-war environment, offered a politics of grievance fuelled by continuing austerity and held a number of assemblies in the later 1940s. Perhaps more importantly, the cross-party consensus seemed at least plausible. Many Scottish Liberal and Labour politicians had an historic and frequently an instinctive attraction to home rule. Scottish Unionists, as the architects of administrative devolution, made a principled stand against 'centralisation' from the opposition benches and in Scottish constituencies.[50]

The question of how to respond to nationalist claims had been largely responsible for ending Westwood's tenure at the Scottish Office and it was clear that one of Woodburn's central tasks was to resolve the situation.[51] He engaged in consultation with members of the Scottish Office, experts on parliamentary procedure and, crucially, Herbert Morrison, who was Lord President of the Council, Deputy Prime Minister and a key architect of Labour's domestic programme. He also met with MacCormick and a deputation from the committee of the Scottish National Assembly in 1948, a meeting during which MacCormick formed a characteristically unfavourable opinion of Woodburn: 'a typical party bureaucrat, efficient, uninspired and totally incapable of looking at anything except through the narrow eyes of party bias'.[52]

As with many of MacCormick's other caustic judgements, this one was unfair. Woodburn took the issue seriously and in December 1947, before meeting the Assembly deputation, he presented a memorandum for cabinet discussion containing his assessment of public opinion and of possible actions. His assessment of the party-political situation was that, because all parties were involved to some degree in the discussion of home rule, there was a justification for action. More importantly, he attempted to pin down where the large body of public opinion rested. It was not the first and would not be the last effort to move beyond the demands of the SNP ('picturesque and articulate' but with

[49] J. Mitchell, *Strategies for Self-government: The Campaigns for a Scottish Parliament* (Edinburgh, 1996), 85–92.

[50] M. Cragoe, '"We like local patriotism": The Conservative Party and the Discourse of Decentralisation, 1947–51', *English Historical Review*, cxxii (2007), 965–85.

[51] The best analysis of Woodburn's role in these events is found in I. Levitt, 'Britain, the Scottish Covenant movement and devolution, 1946–50', *Scottish Affairs*, xxii (1998), 33–57.

[52] J. M. MacCormick, *The Flag in the Wind: The Story of the National Movement in Scotland* (London, 1955), 126. The other members of the deputation were William Gallacher (former chairman of the Scottish Co-operative Wholesale Society and former president of the Scottish Home Rule Association), James Graham, 6th duke of Montrose (founder member of the Scottish Party and, from 1935, a Liberal) and Andrew Dewar Gibb (jurist, founder member of the Scottish Party and Unionist).

negligible support) and of committed home rulers (larger, but not yet a challenge to existing partisan alignments) to reach 'sensible' public opinion, the 'smouldering pile that might suddenly break through the party loyalties and become a formidable national movement'.[53]

Woodburn's opinion on Labour's historic commitment to home rule had, in common with that of other socialists, been cooling for some time – not least on the basis of economic arguments derived from Scotland's interwar experiences – and James Mitchell identifies Woodburn as the least sympathetic to home rule of Labour's three post-war Scottish Secretaries.[54] He put to the cabinet a number of measures, which were later embodied in a white paper: alterations to parliamentary procedure to allow for the second reading of 'Scottish' bills and some autonomous discussion of the Scottish estimates to be done by the Scottish Grand Committee and the establishment of a Scottish Economic Conference chaired by the Secretary of State to discuss Scottish issues. Any suggestions of a wide-ranging inquiry had been parked because of the difficulties of establishing a sensible remit and the likelihood of an inquiry sustaining nationalist agitation rather than calming it. Similarly, further administrative devolution or any commitments to site nationalised industries in Scotland were dismissed.[55]

If Woodburn had not, in the first instance, regarded the home rule agitation as 'a Tory plot to embarrass the Socialist government', his approach to the issue did become more and more trenchant during his period as Secretary of State. One reason was that MacCormick's efforts to defeat Labour in the Paisley by-election (a month after his meeting with Woodburn) as a 'National' candidate with Liberal and Unionist support, was accompanied by bitter attacks on the menace of 'state socialism'.[56] This raised the partisan temperature around the issue of home rule and further alienated Woodburn and other Labour politicians. Labour's victory in Paisley was also an eloquent reminder that, while home rule might garner wide support, it was the top priority for only a comparatively small number of activists and voters. The mass petitioning Covenant campaign that followed, a return to pressure group tactics, was colourful and widespread, but Woodburn

[53] National Archives, Cabinet Papers, CAB/129/22, 'Scottish Demands for Home Rule or Devolution: Memorandum by the Secretary of State for Scotland', 6 December 1947.
[54] Mitchell, *Strategies for Self-government*, 147.
[55] Scottish Home Department, *Scottish Affairs*, Cmd 7308 (London, 1948).
[56] M. Dyer, '"A Nationalist in the Churchillian Sense": John MacCormick, the Paisley By-election of 18 February 1948, Home Rule and the Crisis in Scottish Liberalism', *Parliamentary History*, xxii (2003), 285–307.

could justifiably rest on the ground of having pursued all reasonable and practical measures available.

His argument that he could not be accused of having done nothing did not, of course, placate nationalist criticism. If he had not begun his office with a narrowly partisan outlook, in the face of the Covenant campaign, he quickly developed one. This was underpinned not only by Unionist efforts to address the Convention's grievances, but also support for the Covenant among groups with whom Woodburn had previously locked horns: the ILP and the Communist Party in particular. His attitudes towards the question were revealed privately in a letter to the man who would succeed him as Scottish Secretary, Hector McNeil, in November 1949. It was a letter of reassurance: the nationalist threat had been overplayed in the press; as an issue, it had 'receded in relative importance' when set next to the international situation and the continuing challenges of reconstruction; and the Scottish Labour party itself now had a clear line, having rejected a motion for an inquiry into home rule at its annual conference.[57]

When he made similar points in a heated address debate two days later they were accompanied by more controversial material. His arguments that parliamentary devolution involved fundamental constitutional issues and that both the domestic and international contexts (the Soviet Union had exploded its first atomic bomb in August) were not suited to lengthy and destabilising inquiries in preference to incremental and pragmatic tinkering were unexceptional. These arguments would underpin Labour's official policy into the 1960s. As Woodburn laid into the heterogeneity of the supporters of the Covenant movement, taking particular aim at communist and Marxist support, he turned on MacCormick:

> Even the leader of this movement during a very critical point in our affairs made a speech which suggested that the only way Scotland would get justice would be if somebody threw a bomb on Downing Street. I saw another speech of his recently in which on three occasions he mentioned the word "bomb". Now, in these emotional movements that is very dangerous talk, and we have already had experience of bombs being in existence in this movement on two separate occasions in Scotland.[58]

MacCormick's recollection that 'Woodburn's gunpowder plot ... was headlined in every Scottish newspaper and ... made him

---

[57] NLS, Woodburn Papers, Box 1/1, AW to Hector McNeill, 14 November 1949.
[58] *Parliamentary Debates* (Commons), 469, 16 November 1949, col. 2097.

a laughing-stock throughout the length and breadth of the land' overstates the impact of the intervention.[59] Undoubtedly, however, the unwelcome attention that the speech did draw to the Covenant movement formed part of the context for Attlee's decision, following Labour's slim election victory in February 1950, to shift Woodburn to the Ministry of Fuel and Power and replace him at the Scottish Office with the press-savvy Hector McNeil.

It was an inglorious end to a tenure at the Scottish Office which, if judged by UK government expenditure on Scottish housing, health and energy, was otherwise a considerable success.[60] Woodburn declined the offer of a move to the Fuel and Power and returned instead to the backbenches. However privately incensed he was by Attlee's decision, he remained characteristically loyal in public, circulating a letter to his constituents explaining his exit as the simple by-product of the need to reorganise and refresh the government.[61]

After Government

Woodburn was not to achieve high office again and, indeed, his draft autobiography ends at the period shortly after his ejection from the Scottish Office. He was reinstated as the Labour spokesman on Scottish affairs during the 1950s. He continued to make the case against parliamentary devolution both in parliamentary speeches and in the press and remained wary of nationalist politics.[62] He assembled a large dossier of notes, papers and clippings on nationalist movements in the 1950s and 60s, the better to refute and combat nationalist arguments. As late as 1967, in the immediate aftermath of SNP victory at the Hamilton by-election, he wrote to the Lord Advocate, Henry Wilson, for information on all incidents in which nationalist political groups had used violence or been found collecting weapons.[63] In Woodburn's trajectory, the historian can trace the rapidity and completeness of Labour alienation from home rule and nationalism in the years around the Second World War.

Woodburn remained a model parliamentarian. He was a conscientious attender and a frequent parliamentary speaker. He spoke

[59]   MacCormick, *Flag in the Wind*, 133.
[60]   Levitt, 'Scottish Covenant Movement', 46–7.
[61]   'Mr Woodburn and the Cabinet', *Alloa Advertiser*, 11 March 1950.
[62]   See, for example, 'Scots Self-Government' and 'Scotland's "Fruitful Partnership" with England', *Edinburgh Evening News*, 3 and 16 January 1952; *Parliamentary Debates* (Commons), 753, 1 November 1967, cols 201–10.
[63]   NLS, Woodburn Papers, Box 16/2, Henry Wilson to AW, 5 December 1967.

knowledgeably in areas where he felt he had some expertise and sat, for example, on the Select Committee on Procedure from 1956 to 1968. His interest in education he sustained through enthusiastic support for and advice on Harold Wilson's plans for the Open University in the 1960s.[64]

He developed other interests as well as contributing in areas where he felt his previous experiences and aptitudes made his perspective valuable. One new commitment, whose beginnings feature in the autobiography, was his involvement in the British Inter-parliamentary Union. He led the delegation to the Federal Republic of Germany in 1951 and he subsequently led delegations to Uruguay, Spain, Uganda and Kenya. His linguistic abilities suited him to this kind of diplomacy and it was a role he clearly relished.[65]

His instinctive cosmopolitanism along with his economic literacy also underpinned his early advocacy (rare among Scottish Labour MPs) for British membership of the European Economic Community.[66] His last substantial parliamentary intervention was on this topic, in a debate on the Wilson government's White Paper offering an economic assessment of British entry to the Common Market. As a man in his late seventies, Woodburn drew on his experiences of the interwar years, on his own understanding of nationality, and on an optimistic internationalism to make the case:

> I believe that there is no danger in our going into Europe. The idea that all the horrible things that have been suggested will happen the day after we join the Common Market is belied by history. I am a member of a small country which has been a member of the greatest common market in the world for 250 years. It has not lost its identity. The Scots are still Scots … It is a great ideal, this brotherhood of man in the world. It is the ideal of organising the unity of Europe with a view to preventing further wars and dictatorships, a view not only of a Europe contributing to the well-being of the backward countries but of organising Europe economically and militarily. I hope that all this will lead to the wonderful and colourful variety of the constituent parts of Europe contributing to the future culture of the world. We all – Frenchmen, Germans, Irish, Welsh, Scots and English and the rest – have a wonderful colourful variety of experience and gifts and

[64] NLS, Woodburn Papers, Box 1/2, Harold Wilson to AW, 9 October 1963 and 30 November 1964.
[65] NLS, Woodburn Papers, Boxes 7–8.
[66] NLS, Woodburn Papers, Acc. 7656, Box 12/2; AW, *A Commonsense View of the Common Market: A Personal Statement* (London, n.d.).

it is that variety that makes Europe the wonder and marvel of the world.[67]

Towards the end of his career, in reviewing David Maxwell Fyfe's memoirs, Woodburn assessed political memoirs as a genre: 'Politicians who write their autobiographies are always in difficulties. The one person they are likely to appraise wrongly is the author.'[68] While his own autobiography is, of course, subject to the same partialities and positioned viewpoints as those of any such effort, he seems largely to have avoided the pitfall he identified. His assessment of himself and his own career rings true. In preserving it, he offers the reader a unique perspective on Scottish political history for the first two thirds of the twentieth century.

---

[67] *Parliamentary Debates* (Commons), 796, 25 February 1970, cols 1288–94.
[68] 'Personalities and Politics', *Edinburgh Evening News*, 30 April 1964.

EDITORIAL CONVENTIONS

Various versions of Woodburn's autobiography exist within his papers (National Library of Scotland, Acc. 7656). Box 4 contains four versions of mixed manuscript and typescript materials. The overriding aim in this edition has been to assemble a full edited and readable version of the text. It is principally assembled from two of the versions within Woodburn's papers. Version 1 is the full first draft of the autobiography covering the years from 1890 to 1951. It is richly annotated but contains large numbers of typographical errors, considerable extraneous detail, and a good deal of repetition. Version 4 is a revised version of the first part of the first draft up to Woodburn's experience of the 1929 general election as a candidate for South Edinburgh.

The text that follows is a combination of two of these versions (1 and 4). Chapters 1 to 6 offer a full edited text of version 4 of the autobiography. Additions, which are indicated by the use of square brackets, are from version 1. These are inserted where Woodburn gave more detailed information about a particular recollection in the full first draft, or where he included material of historical interest which was subsequently left out of the revised version 4. Chapters 7 to 10 offer a full edited text of the remainder of the unrevised first draft. Additions in these chapters, again indicated by square brackets, are from version 3 of the autobiography, in which Woodburn offered slightly more detail on the activities undertaken as secretary of the Labour Party in Scotland.

In the interest of creating a clean and readable text, straightforward spelling and typographical errors have been silently corrected throughout, capitalisation has been made consistent and commas and other punctuation have been inserted as appropriate. Purely factual errors have been left intact. The different versions of the autobiography made only very sparing use of paragraphs and of chapter breaks. The edited version has indented paragraphs as appropriate and broken the work into chapters.

ABBREVIATIONS

AW	Arthur Woodburn
BSISLP	British Section of the International Socialist Labour Party
BSP	British Socialist Party
CO	Conscientious Objector
CP	Communist Party
CPGB	Communist Party of Great Britain
CWC	Clyde Workers' Committee
DCM	District Court Martial
ILP	Independent Labour Party
MFGB	Miners' Federation of Great Britain
NCLC	National Council of Labour Colleges
NLS	National Library of Scotland
PPS	Parliamentary Private Secretary
RC	Roman Catholic
SDF	Social Democratic Federation
SHRA	Scottish Home Rule Association
SLC	Scottish Labour College
SLP	Socialist Labour Party
SNP	Scottish National Party
SSP	Scottish Socialist Party
STUC	Scottish Trades Union Congress
TUC	Trades Union Congress
UF	United Free
USSR	Union of Soviet Socialist Republics
WEA	Workers Educational Association

THE AUTOBIOGRAPHY OF
ARTHUR WOODBURN
1890–1978

CHAPTER ONE

It was interesting to watch Winston Churchill[1] during the war. He not only felt he was taking part in great events, he was conscious in his every act that he was helping to shape them. In his speeches he was writing history in the making. On quite another plane my own life has been closely bound up with other events which have greatly influenced world history and made a revolution in the lives ordinary men and women have to lead.

I was born in 1890 about the time when the Labour Party was first formed in Scotland and I have been privileged to see its rise to power and play some little part in its achievements. At the beginning it was a protest against social injustice, poverty, unnecessary illness, and denial to the mass of the people of opportunity to live full lives. It became the spearhead of a universal movement to create a world nearer to the heart's desire. At one moment about 1948, it became possible to say of Great Britain that for the first time in any country there was no need for any child to go hungry or be denied the opportunity to develop to the full all the gifts with which nature had endowed it. The ideals of its pioneers, that society could and should be planned to provide prosperity for all, had been accepted as national policy and the development of technology made this possible, depending only on the will of men to agree on the principles and means to achieve the end in practice.

Robert Owen[2] had coined the name 'socialism' – the state of being social – to describe this ideal but though the evangelical wing of the Labour movement accepted this aim it was not until 1918 that the Labour Party adopted it as an official policy. Most trade unionists were still Liberal or Tory and the inclusion of socialism in the constitutional aims of trade unionism was a propaganda victory for the Independent Labour Party which was the driving force of progressive ideas. The

---

[1] Sir Winston Leonard Spencer Churchill (1874–1965), writer, politician and Prime Minister.
[2] Robert Owen (1771–1858), industrialist, philanthropist and pioneer socialist.

trade union movement itself remained largely an organisation to struggle for better wages and defend workers' rights.

Since my own life has been so involved with these developments which have changed the face of our civilisation it may be of interest to record some recollections which will throw some light on a great social revolution. My father was born in Kilmarnock in the year 1842. His father was a weaver and his forebears, I believe, were farmers. He moved to Lasswade, near Edinburgh, to be employed in the carpet works there. In later life he came to Edinburgh to work as a customs officer, charging tolls on the cattle and sheep which passed along Fountainbridge on the way to the Grassmarket. My mother was born in Slateford on the west side of the city. [Her name was Janet Brown and there was a tradition in her family that they were descended from John Brown of Priesthill who was shot at his door by Claverhouse in the troubled days of the Covenanters.] Her father was a 'captain' in charge of Stoneyport, one of the stopping places on the Union Canal which had been built to connect Edinburgh and Glasgow. In the then state of the roads this was the best and quickest way of transport between the two cities. Cargo was carried in barges but for passengers there was an express service of 'swift boats' pulled by horses which trotted or galloped along the bank. These stopped at the various ports to change horses and provide refreshments. The canal terminated in Edinburgh at a basin which was later drained to become the site of Lothian House. Edinburgh in earlier times was a kind of Venice of little lochs at intervals from the end of the canal down to the sea. Near the canal basin was Lochrin where the barges were built. There was a further loch where the Meadows replaced it and the Nor Loch which is now Princes Street Gardens. Loch End, St Margarets and other water areas continued the line down to Portobello.

Education in Scotland had been established after the reformation by the new church and from then on the ordinary people had access to knowledge and an open channel from the cottage to the university. It was in a church school that my father received his education. By the time I was born he had a small brass foundry near our house. This with its moulding sand became my playground and from my earliest years I was absorbing the language of the workshop and listening to the problems of workmen and industry.

This familiarity with the practical side of life was to serve me well in later life when I became involved in industrial life and commerce, as MP and then as a minister of aircraft and engineering. The language of industry was as valuable to me in discussions with industrialists and trade unions as is a knowledge of foreign languages in international affairs. It is a mistake in my view to separate education from real living and it is good that children should participate in affairs from the earliest age. Nothing can give in later life the real feel of the farm, the workshop, medicine and even military life which comes from living in a home with their respective traditions. It is probably better to add the general broad education to such grass roots background than at a less receptive age to add the specialised knowledge to a general knowledge with no clear roots. Heredity and tradition are valuable assets to the effectiveness of man. Even if the miner's son becomes a scientist or the carpenter's son becomes a surgeon the intimate acquaintance with craftsmanship in earlier life remains a valuable asset. It also helps to balance the disastrous tendency to glorify the so-called white collar jobs. Art is not confined to painting on canvas and though there was still a suggestion of 'gentlemen and players' in the ceremony, it was a sign of progress when at the unveiling of the monument to King George at Westminster they honoured the mason who had worked with the architect in its construction. All our homes and buildings owe their beauty to the art of craftsmen and workmen as well as to their designers. Education should utilise every interest and activity of the child.

My first school was Bruntsfield public school, then a pioneer model school. It had a first class gymnasium and swimming pool. It anticipated the modern ideal by being a comprehensive school which took the pupil from infant class to the university as happened to several of my classmates. I progressed from Bruntsfield to Boroughmuir higher grade school, another pioneering development. This was situated on the edge of Bruntsfield Links which with Leith Links have the honour of being the first places where modern golf was played. Golf and football are two of Scotland's contributions to sport and friendly rivalries between people which give a peaceful outlet to animosities which frequently lead to strife and war [sic].

I was a bright enough student but not a great one. In my day my elders found it just as difficult to assist me in the advancing lessons of my school as do parents of today with their children engrossed in electronics and computers. Children brought up in homes where there is a tradition of study have a great advantage over those who have to find their own way in the techniques of learning. My home had no background of academics but an atmosphere of craft and pride of workmanship. Moreover I must confess that I fell in with the code of my schoolmates who considered boys were 'soft' who studied and worked hard at their lessons.

In geometry we were usually asked in turn to prove a proposition and according to where we sat in the class we could have time during the process to learn up the lesson before our turn came. I was caught out one morning. The teacher reached me before I had had time to finish my preparation. I started according to the book but after I had reached the limits of my preparation I found myself on my own. By some miracle I proved the proposition but not strictly according to the book. To my surprise I found I was regarded as some sort of prodigy and acquired a reputation for logic which later became an embarrassment. The headmaster and my teacher were both keen mathematicians and thenceforth I was produced as a star turn to demonstrate my prowess. Had I done my homework on the first occasion I would have avoided much later effort in sustaining a reputation which was none of my seeking.

This cult of avoiding learning landed me in another trap. We were offered the choice of starting a course of Latin or taking advanced English. Under the mistaken impression that I already knew English, this seemed the way to an easy life. I soon found that my shortcomings were revealed and I had to work harder than I would have had to do if I had chosen Latin. However I never forgot the English I did learn though I began to understand my own language better as I proceeded with the study of foreign languages. Essays were my bugbear. I could write all I knew about bees and nature on a half a sheet of notepaper and the flowery descriptions of my more gifted schoolmates had my most profound admiration. Curiously enough, when I started work in an office where I was plunged into the writing of business letters I found myself congratulated on the conciseness and clarity of my writing.

I started in this office on the day I became fourteen years of age – the earliest I could leave school. This was not, then, because I wanted to leave off learning. On the contrary, I had become interested and actually started on further education that same night by enrolling in a night school. What happened was that I was pressed into going to work and was actually reluctant to give up the five years' course on which I had embarked. My father had died when I was nine years of age. He was only fifty-seven. He had begun the building of a new foundry but he never lived to use it. My oldest brother was living at home having lost his wife. He ran the business side of the foundry while at times three other brothers were engaged on the practical side.

In my childhood the foundry had an unending interest for me and I liked to work in it. I delivered small castings to various engineering works and gained acquaintance with these. I myself moulded small castings and in the early mornings before I went to school I used to go down and clean out the crucible furnaces. No one asked me to do this but I felt I was really playing a part. Before this I had taken a job to deliver morning rolls at 2/6 a week. I suppose all this used up some of the energy which might have found its outlet in 'juvenile delinquency' of which I have no doubt I had my share.

I think also, the domestic circumstances gave me a sense of responsibility and saddled me with problems which for some people never occur at all and for others arise only at a more mature age. Being the last of a big family, by the time I was growing up, the older generation was dying out and I was having a periodical and close acquaintance with death and funerals. I had with the rest of the family the duty of paying my last respects to the deceased. We passed round him or her in the coffin where the body rested in its white sheet and frills. I was able to appreciate the story of Lady Leslie Mackenzie[3] who told of the boy rescued from the slums by Barnardo's Homes. He had been taken to the home, duly bathed and put to bed with his white sheet tucked up to his chin. When she asked him how he felt he replied 'I've never been deid before!' It is difficult in these days of a welfare state to realise the kind of poverty and misery in which large numbers of people existed. Although I am glad to say that our family were not directly affected, I can, for example, still recall processions of unemployed masons passing through our street and collecting from people almost as poor as themselves. They had long bamboo poles with collecting baskets which reached to the top windows of the tenements. There was no such thing as unemployment benefit. Many of them suffered from silicosis, called the masons' disease, or consumption. Soup kitchens were opened by the churches. People were supplied with a bowl of soup and a piece of bread for I think 1d.

I once referred to these times at a meeting in Inverkeithing with the local provost in the chair. Explaining that so common was it for infants to die in the first years of their lives that parents, as one of their first acts, had to insure their newly borns in a funeral society to make sure they would have a 'decent burial', failure to do so was the ultimate disgrace. I went on to relate that it was because of this custom that I got my Christian name. The family names had all been exhausted before I appeared and while my father and mother were discussing the possibilities a knock came to the door and it happened to be the 'insurance man' calling for his subscriptions. His name was Arthur and so I became Arthur. I commented to the meeting that this was a bit of luck. It might, I said, have been Ebenezer. The whole audience rocked with laughter. Though I did not know, the provost's name was Ebenezer!

---

[3]   Dame Helen Carruthers Mackenzie [*née* Spence] (1859–1945), educationist and public health campaigner.

In working-class districts there were few facilities for children to play. The drying green surrounded by the tenements was the only safe place. There soon was little 'green' left. It was usually hard mud. The alternative was the street. There was of course less traffic and it is incredible to think how many accidents there were from carts and buses drawn by horses. The other danger spot for children was the Union Canal. I recall about 1905 that it was frozen for a long period and skaters could travel about fifteen miles along its surface. On a still earlier occasion my mother told me of it being quite a fairground with stalls selling refreshments along the banks. Another game of the period was street battles between the Scots and the Irish. Gangs of boys took opposite sides and battered each other with hard paper balls attached to sticks. One could have understood their wanting to fight the English as their historical enemy but why the Irish? It was certainly an Irish way of celebrating St Patrick's Day – having a fight for the fun of it.

It was the 'gay nineties' and theatres were much in evidence. In my district they ranged from a tiny one called 'The Gaff' in Dalry Road to a rather bigger one in 'The Grove' and Edinburgh's Drury Lane – the Lyceum in Grindlay Street. They played the melodramas then in vogue. In one of these I recall a thrilling scene where the villain tied the heroine to a travelling belt which was carrying her into a machine to suffer a horrible death. This was more than a sailor in the audience could stand. He jumped on the stage, knocked the villain out and rescued the girl from her terrible fate.

My school days came to an end rather unexpectedly. A cousin of about the same age as myself had gone to work in a lawyer's office [Simpson and Marwick, the lawyers for the Free Church of Scotland]. I had engaged at school to go on to a pre-university course and was now definitely interested in learning. This was 1904 when there was a nationwide crisis arising out of the splitting of the then great Free Church in Scotland. A section had refused to agree with the decision to unite with the United Presbyterian Church and insisted that the huge majority had left the Free Church and that therefore all the property and other assets of the original church remained their property. This became a big legal battle which eventually was decided in the House of Lords.

The objectors who held on to the rump of the Free Church appointed a secretary, J. Hay Thorburn,[4] a member of an Edinburgh legal firm, to be the commander of the 'Wee Free' forces in the campaign. It was virtually a bitter civil war. In every parish the two churches were lined up. Large congregations found themselves excluded from their

---

[4]   John Hay Thorburn (d.1931), businessman and Free Church leader.

churches and small groups of dissenters took possession of the church property. While all this was the law, the results caused such confusion and obvious injustice that Parliament had to intervene and eventually a royal commission was appointed to adjudicate and make a reasonable allocation of the assets to each of the contending parties. My cousin was bringing material regularly from the main legal office to Hay Thorburn and on one of these visits, Thorburn asked him if he knew of any boy like himself who could come and work for him. My name was suggested and I was doomed. Thorburn never gave up until I had left school and become the third member of his staff. This consisted of a clerk, a typist and myself as office boy and general everything. The clerk eventually became the Secretary of the Edinburgh Chamber of Commerce. Curiously enough, my own connections were with the United Free Church.

It was a great experience. I spent the first part of my working life in the midst of a terrific political battle which disturbed the life of Scotland for some years. It produced giants of church politics and I heard passionate oratory of a higher order than is normally heard in Parliament. There were great voices, high intelligence and deep conviction. During this period I had little of the normal life of a boy. My Saturday afternoons were often employed sending out campaign circulars to MPs and others. Our small organisation managed wonderfully well to combat the much larger and more powerful organisation of the United Free Church.

One of the first fruits of victory was that the United Free Church had to hand over all the property in Edinburgh to the Free Church. We took it over. There must have been few such occasions in history. J. Hay Thorburn, Charles W. Bell, Miss Shearer the typist and myself went in solemn procession from the office in 130 George Street to the top of the Mound where we took possession of the offices with 400 rooms with a telephone in each and the West Assembly Hall with the adjacent New College. The four of us moved in as the new government. As the aide-de-camp of the commander I had to interview everyone who came and was in practice, in modern parlance, the public relations officer. Our staff began to grow. Almost unknown ministers arrived from far away parishes to take over the various jobs. The press relied upon me to keep them informed about all the new personalities who began to come into the limelight. For example, one minister from Biggar in Lanarkshire and another from Lamlash in Arran suddenly found themselves professors in the New College.

The bitterness and hatred displayed in this controversy did much to shake my faith in churchianity. I found that many ministers of religion behaved to each other with less charity than one was accustomed to from one's neighbours. In some cases I was shocked by the intolerance and even unscrupulous methods employed by Christian leaders to secure their ends. One example of this was when the Rev. Alexander Lee[5] opened a letter addressed to J. Hay Thorburn which had wrongly been addressed to the UF [United Free] offices and used its contents in the public controversy. Hay Thorburn made such a row about it that in the end Lee had to resign his offices in the Church. He was a tremendous figure, with a leonine head, powerful voice, and a powerful debater.

[There were some fine Christians among the ministers in both Churches but I was shocked by the unscrupulous and cruel way this battle was conducted and this feeling, later reinforced by the Churches' attitude to war, considerably shook my, until then, strong adherence to organised religion. As one illustration of the depth of feeling in these days I recall the Rev. Murdo McQueen's[6] denunciation of the pipe organ in the Free North Church which had been loaned to us for our Assembly. Shaking his fist towards it he declaimed: 'And that abominable thing, I would grind it to powder or bury it for ever in the depths of the German ocean.']

This church experience came alive again nearly twenty-five years later. The Independent Labour Party having successfully brought the trades unions over to socialism, and the Labour Party having become the Government of the country, the ILP had achieved its purpose and there was no point in its lingering on the stage. It had been the driving force of the Labour Party, it had provided it with its policy and personalities and to remain as a separate party was to waste effort in duplication. It became evident also that to justify the existence of a separate party one had to have a separate policy and separate leaders. So logically the ILP decided to merge itself in the Labour Party.

A minority objected and before the decision was reached I was consulted by one of the largest ILP branches in central Edinburgh who were worried what they would do with their hall and funds. I realised from the case of the Wee Frees that the same law would apply and warned them that unless they transferred their property either to trustees or to the Labour Party before the ILP dissolved, all their property would pass to any dissenters. They accepted my advice but unfortunately they were dissuaded from acting on it by their general Secretary – Arthur Brady[7] – who I think had already

---

[5]   Rev. Alexander Lee (1848–1919), Free Church minister, ordained 1872.
[6]   Rev. Murdo Macqueen, Free Church minister from 1884 to his death in 1912, Moderator of the Free Church 1904.
[7]   Arthur Brady (d. 1954), Labour activist, ILP member and founder of Scottish Socialist Party, of which he became secretary.

contemplated forming a successor party to the ILP, which he later did. As a consequence, when the ILP joined with the Labour Party all the property and funds of the central branch and many others passed to the odd members who decided to carry on as the ILP. In the case of the central branch there were, I believe, only two or three, one of whom had only joined in recent weeks.

Throughout Scotland the disaster was no less shattering in its way than in the case of the church dispute. Men and women who had worked for thirty and forty years building up the ILP saw everything they had built up handed over in some cases to a few individuals who made no real use of it. This was also a great blow to the Labour Party. Long standing members of the ILP who had given great service and who would have carried on as members although their careers had taken them into other spheres, or who had become supporters rather than workers, were disheartened and left the movement altogether. Throughout Scotland this was especially serious for in many places there was no Labour Party – only the ILP, and the loss of the key personnel meant that there was little foundation upon which to build the new Party. That, however, is a later part of my story.

At home there was concern for my future. The family council – my mother and older brothers – felt that I should follow my inclinations and become an engineer. The idea was that I should be apprenticed to a small general engineer where I would learn every branch of the trade. My oldest brother dissented. He said no one got anywhere in modern society who took his coat off to work. A draughtsman seemed a reasonable compromise and I started applying for jobs. I was offered one but as the firm demanded a premium and my brothers held the idea that I should be paid for working, I had to decline. My applications seemed to meet with approval and I took one with a firm of engineers and iron founders – Miller and Company. The job had been advertised at three times the salary I was paid by the church – £16 a year – but the firm had been looking for someone older. However they found me satisfactory and offered me the job at £30 a year. This was the beginning of a service which lasted twenty-five years. I hope I did well. I gratefully acknowledge how well they served me.

They gave every encouragement to anyone who wanted to learn and I had often gaps of time in which I was able to study. These were mainly languages which I used in my work. The firm sent goods to nearly every country in the world. Its chilled-iron wheels were running in towns as far apart as St Petersburg and Tokyo. There was regular correspondence in German, French and Spanish. I knew French very well – one of the reasons for my getting the job – and I was also attending classes in German at Heriot-Watt College – later

University. In Miller's, the secretary of the Company conducted all the foreign correspondence and when he was absent I became the deputy. My German was not yet very good and I sometimes ran into difficulties when letters arrived from Germany written in the old hand script. It was difficulty enough to decipher normal German words in bad handwriting but when the words were highly technical, it became a tour de force for the combined efforts of the manager and myself to get the meaning. It is inconceivable these days that correspondence from important firms abroad could come in handwritten letters. At that time, before typewriters were the order of the day, such letters were registered by being copied into letter books whose thin paper absorbed under a letter press the special ink in which they were written.

It was one of the mistakes of the old methods of teaching languages that it was seldom made clear to students that a language is not just adding words together and building up sentences like a meccano set, but that language is idiomatic and one has to learn how people actually speak and write it. The less one knows of a language the more important it is to have a full and comprehensive dictionary. Even with my imperfect German I found this to be true in carrying out a propaganda campaign I engaged in to gain an entrance for one of our products to the German market.

The 1924 General Election was fought largely on relations with Russia. The Labour Government had concluded a trade agreement with Russia which gave us advantages over the limits of our fishermen and the sale of our herring. This made a useful scare coming after all the aftermath of the revolution and the invasion wars with the Bolsheviks. At the end the decisive blow was struck by the publication on the eve of the voting of the 'Zinoviev' letter forgery and the Tories won another term of office. They had to back up this propaganda by some action and they curtailed loans to Russia which were to promote mutual trade. At that time Russia had been negotiating to buy papermaking machinery from Britain in the manufacture of which we excelled. Securing the first orders meant also that we had a continual follow-up of orders for replacements and future developments. This opportunity was lost. The irony of the situation was that the Russians promptly turned to Germany and as Germany could get the credits from us, we still financed the Russian paper mills, but Germany got the orders. Miller's supplied one of the important components of these great machines – the rolls for the calendering or polishing of the paper. Our men had the know-how and our chilled iron rolls were the most reliable in the world. We had only two normal competitors – Krupp's of Germany and Farrel Foundry in the States. It was therefore something of a triumph that though this country lost the order for the complete machine, our firm in Edinburgh were able to get the order from the Germans for the calendar rolls. However in my initial campaign to break into the German market I made full use of the idiomatic translations of my excellent dictionary and we won our first order.

Our firm seldom had any complaints and the work and quality of our products was usually first class but as luck would have it, something went wrong with the goods supplied and my German was severely taxed to carry on the argument which followed. Eventually our chief engineer and the managing director had to visit Germany to settle the matter. The Germans asked our delegation where Mr Scott – the director who had signed the correspondence – had lived when he was in Germany. Our chairman did not know what they were talking about and replied that he did not think Scott had ever been in Germany. The Germans said that he could not have written such letters without having lived in Germany. This was a great compliment to my Cassell's German dictionary.

Spanish I did not know at that time and it was a necessary language for our work. So I advised another junior to take up Spanish as I had enough on my plate learning French and German. He was a bit shy so I offered to take up Spanish with him but was clear in my own mind that I could not do much work at it. It was a class of about forty being taught on the Berlitz system – that is, nothing but Spanish from the start. The class, like all classes, dwindled during the long session and finished with an attendance of four. My friend had dropped out long ago. I carried on for several years. This system left me with a feeling of being at home with Spanish which was not the case with German where the teaching was more academic and literary.

It is interesting that in all my classes I learned far more than the language. Le Harivel,[8] who taught us French, also taught us to think like Frenchman and to love the country and its people. He argued for its politics and customs. He even discussed the issue of capital punishment which had been hotly debated in the French parliament. I always remembered the French Deputy who declared he was in favour of the abolition of capital punishment but, said he, 'let the murderers commence'. Max Salas,[9] my Spanish teacher, got very heated when everyone was talking about German aggression and gave us a long lecture on the example of British imperialism in Gibraltar which he naturally held to be a part of Spain. So this subject had a familiar ring when it became a live issue fifty years later. My German teacher –

[8] Charles S. Le Harivel (d. 1925), teacher of French at Edinburgh Ladies' College, Heriot-Watt College and the Free Church Training College.
[9] Head of the Pictorial School of Languages, 7 South Charlotte Street, Edinburgh.

Dallas[10] – was a Scots minister who had lived and married in Germany. His wife was the sister of the German ambassador in Rome and he was well versed in German history, politics and policies. He told us, for example, how the Germans used convicts from their prisons to recover peat land for agriculture, how the German language owed its start to the necessity of Luther finding a vehicle for carrying his bible to the people. One of the text books we had for translation included long passages from Bellamy's *Looking Backward*[11] which gave me a lesson in the immorality of the existing social system and the possibility of an ideal socialist society. Education, like peach, is indivisible. Nye Bevan[12] in Mr Attlee's[13] Cabinet pointed out that Russia could not train scientists and engineers and restrict their thinking to these specialist subjects. fifty years later it appears that poets and authors were the only people to give evidence of what seemed a truism.

So, for about twelve years after I left school, I attended classes at night studying languages, accountancy and other commercial subjects. Later economics was added to the business studies and it became a life study. I had always been interested in politics. My family were active Liberals and I can recall working hard as a boy of ten in the Khaki [by-]election of 1900 in West Edinburgh where Arthur Dewar fought General Wauchope.[14] I used to have to read the newspaper aloud to my father – who died when I was nine – and I listened and took an interest in the discussions he had at home with friends about the politics of the day and especially the war. I knew all the Scots who had been Prime Ministers and the outstanding politicians, though I had no idea I should ever have any part in these affairs personally. The nation at that time was bitterly divided between those who supported the government and those – mainly Liberals – who opposed the war. They were denounced as pro-Boers. In politics, I was also fortunate in my teachers. Some of them had clearly wider interests than just their own educational subject. At the time of the Japanese-Russian war in 1905 one of my teachers gave us a very interesting lecture on the plans

---

[10] Rev. Alexander Kennedy Dallas (1867–1932), teacher of Latin and German at George Watson's College and Heriot-Watt College.

[11] Edward Bellamy, *Looking Backward, 2000–1887* (Boston, 1888), a utopian science fiction novel, which inspired a socialist movement of so-called 'Nationalist Clubs' in the USA.

[12] Aneurin Bevan (1897–1960), politician and Minister of Health and Housing, 1945–1951.

[13] Clement Richard Attlee (1883–1967), politician and Prime Minister.

[14] AW here must be referring to the by-election for Edinburgh South in June 1899, when Arthur Dewar (1860–1917), fourth son of distiller John Dewar, lawyer and Liberal politician, defeated General Andrew Gilbert Wauchope (1846–1899), an army officer who was killed in December 1899 during the early stages of the South African War.

of the Japanese. These were to begin by invading China, then to move on to Indo China, Burma, Malaya, India, Australia and New Zealand. This was almost the pattern of their successes in the world war over thirty years later in World War Two.

Although I was interested in politics I found it impossible to attend political meetings as they invariably clashed with my classes. On the Friday evenings we had some politics in the college debating society, where the issues of the day were debated by first class speakers. Evolution, Darwin and religion were subjects of great and lively controversy. One of the most eloquent advocates of socialism was the late Will Y. Darling[15] who was later to become one of the most colourful men of his age. He became Lord Provost of Edinburgh at the end of the war and then MP for Edinburgh South. He was really a rather shy person but covered it up by showmanship and aggression. He had a wonderful command of language and used to overwhelm us with flowery eloquence. I myself was more a listener than speaker at these debates. Not that I was inarticulate, for I recall being very active in the arguments of the time and found myself being called on to explain the Liberal policies of taxing land and the increment tax. It is difficult for people nowadays to realise that the differences between individuals at that time over Lloyd George's budgets were absolutely savage compared with the academic disputes of today. I had a friend who was the factor to a large estate in Northumberland and he was rebuked and dismissed for even attending the meeting of the Liberal candidate in an election.

I worked for my new firm for twenty-five years. I had experience in corresponding with several countries in three foreign languages and dealing with trade, exchange and shipping. (Later, on the basis of my interest in economics I became something of an expert in the new idea of costing systems which became fashionable in industry after the First World War.) My interest in economics was set alight when a friend gave me a copy of Ruskin's *Unto This Last* and *Munera Pulveris*.[16] This opened a new world of thought to me and I enrolled in classes on economics in the Heriot-Watt College. My lecturer was William Graham who later became MP for Central Edinburgh and was President of the Board of Trade in Ramsay MacDonald's 1929 Government.[17] We became close friends and in our walks home after

[15] William Young Darling (1885–1962), politician and writer, Lord Provost of Edinburgh 1941–4 and Unionist MP for Edinburgh South, 1945–57.
[16] John Ruskin (1819–1900), art critic and social commentator. His works on political economy, including *Unto this Last* (1862) and *Munera Pulveris* (1872) were influential within British socialism.
[17] William Graham (1887–1932), journalist, ILP activist, Workers Educational As-

the class we discussed many questions of politics and philosophy. A railwayman[18] who used to travel with me regularly in the train I took to my work was an eloquent propagandist for socialism and this seemed the practical application of the moral economics I had imbibed from Ruskin. I became convinced that socialism was the most moral and efficient type of society. Just about this time Normal Angell published his *Great Illusion*[19] and then Brailsford wrote *The War of Steel and Gold*.[20] Both these books opened up a new vista of politics.

In 1911 a cousin who had emigrated to France with his father came with his wife to visit his birth place in Edinburgh. I returned to France with them to spend two weeks at their home in Vailly, a small village near Soissons about forty miles north of Paris. This cousin had been taken to France as a young boy and until the 1914 war, he had kept that habit of the emigrating Scot of remaining in mind a Scot and yet being integrated into the life of his new country. He was a keen observer and used to analyse for me the working of the French mind and he had himself acquired their cynical suspicion of the grandiloquent declarations of politicians. Although I learned later that his disclosures had been made originally in our own Parliament at home, it was from him I heard for the first time about the machinations of the armaments trusts actually provoking crises to stimulate new orders for battleships, guns and munitions.

Sir Charles Beresford,[21] a former British Admiral then an MP, had been carrying on a campaign to get the British army equipped with new rifles and then it was disclosed that he was a director of the firm which supplied the steel for the rifles! I learned how Krupp's, Sneider in France and firms in Britain had engaged in a conspiracy to scare their own governments into spending more money on armaments. While I was in France the conflict among the great powers of these days came to a head. France and Britain had been sharing out the influence and markets in Africa as a practical outcome of the *entente cordiale* by which they had ceased their traditional antagonisms and rivalry. Germany under Kaiser Wilhelm resented being ignored and shutout of the treasure hunt. It brought matters to a head by sending a gunboat into Agadir, a small port in Morocco. France and Britain

sociation (WEA) lecturer on economics and MP for Central Edinburgh 1918–31. Part of Cabinet minority who opposed MacDonald and Snowden's proposed benefit cut in 1931.

[18] Version 3 of the autobiography names this person as William Proudfoot.
[19] Sir Ralph Norman Angell (1872–1967), *The Great Illusion* (1910).
[20] Henry Noel Brailsford (1873–1958), *The War of Steel and Gold* (1914).
[21] Charles William de la Poer Beresford (1846–1919), naval officer and Unionist politician, MP for County Waterford (1874–80), Marylebone East (1885–9), York (1898–1900), Woolwich (1902–3), Portsmouth (1910–16).

were furious and it looked as if war might break out. This gave a more urgent jolt to my developing interest in politics and on my return, I began to read and learn more about diplomacy.

My first holiday in France was not all concerned with politics and I had a happy holiday. I took part in the social life of the village, attended their sports meetings and on the Sunday, left on a cycle tour to the castle of Pierrefonds. We carried on by train to Paris where my cousin established me in a small hotel and left me for the rest of the week to wander round Paris and relive the history of France of which I had been an ardent reader. Before he left we went to a Café Chantant in the Champs Elysees where the violinist who had eloped with the daughter of the Emperor Francis Joseph of Austria was playing to crowded audiences. On my visit to the Louvre I missed seeing the Mona Lisa. It had been stolen the day before and all we saw were the large hooks on which it had been hung. It was recovered some time later in Italy.

CHAPTER TWO

When the war broke out in 1914, in spite of the antagonisms and doubts I had conceived towards the public pronouncements of statesmen, I would have been carried away by the emotional wave which swept the country when Kitchener announced that our country needed us. I was halted because I was in the hands of the doctors and was in and out of Edinburgh Royal Infirmary for investigation of what eventually turned out to be a stone in the kidney. There was also a domestic complication. My father had died when I was nine and left my mother with the small brass-founding business. One of my brothers who had been the mainstay of the affair had left the family foundry to start on his own. The brother remaining in the business had been in the Scots Guards and as a special appeal had been made to such trained men, he went off to the army and this left me with the responsibility for running the foundry and looking after my mother and sister. My mother had no enthusiasm for war. She had seen several wars. As a girl, she remembered the Crimean war. She recalled how when she had to walk from Slateford to attend Edinburgh Royal Infirmary she used to see the soldiers with icicles in their beards during the terrible winter. The family as a whole were not militarily minded. As Liberals they had opposed the Boer War and as a family of artisans there were few military affiliations or traditions.

Where I worked, the firm soon came into contact with the problems which arise. It was genuinely patriotic and ready, like many others, to place itself at the disposal of the nation to win the war. It got orders only to find itself frustrated at every turn. For example, gauges which had to be approved before work was started were held up for months and it was only later discovered that the traditional armament firms had deliberately held these back to protect their monopoly and prevent any newcomers from entering the trade. I began to see the war with new eyes. I attended a meeting addressed by Sir George Paish,[1] the editor of

---

[1]   Sir George Paish (1867–1957), financial journalist, economist and special adviser to David Lloyd George 1909–14.

the *Statist*, and the *Public Trustee*. They appealed to everyone to restrain personal consumption to help the war. I caused some consternation by suggesting that an example might be shown by some of these big firms who were using the war as an opportunity to profiteer. I gave two examples from his own paper. The shipowners were reported to have increased their profits by ten times, from £25 millions to about £250 millions, and the large meat companies had done the same, boasting that they had 'earned' £800 millions in profit. Since the profits of engineering as the result of the Clyde workers' protests had been limited by the government, it seemed to me that stopping profiteering in shipping and food would be a more effective way of achieving economy. This aspect of the war infuriated me – that men and boys should be giving their lives at the front while behind the lines their sacrifices were producing the opportunity for others to amass easy fortunes. This confirmed all the suspicions about the conduct of war which had been raised by my earlier Agadir experiences.

Moreover, in the course of the medical investigations of my ailments the X-Rays in the Royal Infirmary had not been able to detect what was wrong and Dr Hope Fowler,[2] the radiologist, who had become very friendly, suggested that he might be more successful with his private apparatus at his home in Chester Street – Edinburgh's Harley Street of that period. On one Sunday morning I visited him, he had a colleague there and we all discussed the war. It came out in the conversation that the Admiralty had come up to Scotland to make arrangements to open a hospital at Queensferry to deal with war casualties. This visit was in 1912. The Edinburgh doctors had protested at this invasion of their responsibilities in Scotland and eventually the Admiralty agreed that the Scottish doctors would assume the responsibilities. It seemed strange to me that this should be the case when the supposed cause of the war was Germany's decision to invade Belgium in 1914. I was to learn later that Admiral Jacky Fisher[3] already in 1912 had predicted that war would break out in August 1914.

About this time Ramsay MacDonald addressed a meeting in Edinburgh. The press had created the impression that he was a wild and irresponsible person – if not a traitor. I went to hear him. To my surprise, he gave a reasoned and obviously informed analysis of the circumstances that had led up to the war. It became evident that the gauntlet which Germany had thrown down when her gunboat entered

---

[2] Dr William Hope Fowler (1876–1933), radiologist and founder of the Edinburgh School of Radiology.

[3] John Arbuthnot Fisher, first Baron Fisher (1841–1920), naval officer, appointed First Sea Lord in 1904, retired from the admiralty in 1910, but returned as First Sea Lord in 1914 before resigning in May 1915.

Agadir had been lifted then and that the intervening period had been the build-up for the war in 1914, which started at the time forecast by Jacky Fisher. I found MacDonald both interesting and inspiring. The cumulative effect of all these experiences was to make me determined, so far as lay in my power, to fight against the evils of war and this war in particular. George Lansbury,[4] who was editing the *Clarion,* took up an anti-war attitude. By this time I had joined the Independent Labour Party and it also decided to oppose the war. It is difficult for me in retrospect to analyse all the reasons which made me decide to oppose the war but certainly my indignation at the deception of the people about the real issues, the abuse of people's patriotism by unscrupulous profiteering, the refusal of the government to prevent it, and the knowledge of the real causes of the struggle, all combined to forfeit my support.

As an employee of my firm I was classed as an essential worker and when conscription was introduced in 1916 I could not be merely passive and keep out of it, so I wrote to the authorities and declared my opposition to conscription and the war in general. I joined the Anti-conscription League which was closely associated with the No-conscription Fellowship. This latter body was more pacifist than political and had wide support from the Quakers which included the Cadburys. It built up a widespread and efficient organisation throughout the country and proved very embarrassing to the government. We must have appeared a queer collection to those who were busy running the war and they were justifiably irritated by our activities. Any individual has the right to decide according to his conscience what he will or will not willingly do but once a number of individuals combine to carry out activities which are obstructing the carrying out of government policy they become a political organisation. So the campaign of those who opposed conscription was a political campaign. Our attempts to explain to the public our attitude involved us in public controversy.

[I made my first public speech at this time to a huge crowd at the Mound. A few yards away Major Robertson was holding a recruiting meeting. My crowd was largely hostile as there was general enthusiasm and support for the war. Naturally I had no desire to dissuade anyone from joining up who held that view. Indeed I suggested to interrupters they were at the wrong meeting. It must have indeed been an irritation to the major doing his duty and also to those with relatives at the front … These meetings were frequently broken up and one speaker who

---

[4]   George Lansbury (1859-1940), activist, editor and politician, Leader of the Labour Party 1931-5.

took the platform to rescue a minister's wife from a rough handling was himself kicked all the way along Princes Street.]

As a result of my having taken part in public meetings, Major Robertson, the recruiting officer for Edinburgh, mistakenly came to the conclusion that I was the brains behind the war resistance. Pressure was brought to bear on the firm to release me so that I could be called up to the army. The insistence of the head of the firm that I was indispensable naturally confirmed Major Robertson in his exaggerated view of my importance and as it was clearly unfair for me to involve the firm in my attitude and activities I advised the firm to let me go. This they eventually did and at the end of the period prescribed by the law I was arrested, brought before the court and handed over to the military. Major Robertson was very decent about it. He brought a 'brass hat' from the War Office to try and persuade me to drop the whole thing and join up, having made my protest. They said my qualities were needed and all would be forgotten. I fear my obstinacy closed my mind to their well-meant pleas and I spent the next three years in prison. No one quite knew what would be the penalty for refusing to obey orders in war. We certainly had faced up to the possibility of the ultimate penalty and once one had accepted that, any fear of pain or death seemed to disappear. From my experience, I feel that the sufferings of martyrs become sublimated in a kind of ecstasy and that the mind in such cases insulates the brain from the pain our imagination foresees.

The people as a whole had no enthusiasm after a while for war but like Bignold, they said to themselves:

As for war, I go agin it
that is, I kind of sort of do,
but now that us are in it
the best thing is to see it through.

There is, of course, sense in this and I respected those that took this view. I respected the armed forces but resented what I thought was the exploitation of their patriotism, but I felt that someone had to protest. The technique of opposing war was to refuse to obey military orders on the ground that, not having voluntarily enlisted, one was not a soldier. Refusal to obey an order was automatically followed by court martial and conviction could carry the penalty of death. Practically all the penalties in the book were tried on COs to make them comply, including field punishment and sentence of death. A number was actually taken to France and sentenced to death for failure to obey orders in the face of the enemy. This sentence was to have been carried out secretly but the No-conscription Fellowship had built a very efficient organisation which was able to keep track of what was happening in every barracks and every prison where objectors were being held. The sentence of death was raised in Parliament and given national publicity and the carrying out of the death sentence was stopped. The sentence was commuted to life imprisonment. Some actually suffered field punishment and all over the country many varieties of punishments not known to the rule books or to law were given to prisoners. In some barracks the soldiers were sorry for the men and treated them sympathetically. In Scottish regiments COs were treated strictly according to the book with neither leniency nor cruelty. The army in general treated us with respect for standing up for our views. They realised it was no easy matter to defy military orders. I myself received the sensible and quite normal order to clean up the barrack room. I had no quarrel with the other soldiers and it was most difficult to refuse to obey, but as a military order, I had to refuse.

By the time I came under the law, the army had developed a procedure for dealing with COs. I was taken to the COs' office and ordered to put on a pair of army boots. They had a sense of humour for the boots must have been size twelve and they came with me everywhere till the war ended. I refused in front of the witnesses and was formally charged and taken to the guard room. I was kept there for some time till the case was prepared for the court martial. I challenged the validity of the court on the ground that I had never enlisted and was not, therefore, a soldier. The court retired to consider this technical point and proceeded to find me guilty and I was sentenced to fifty-six days' hard labour. In accordance with the procedure I was taken to London to be imprisoned in Wormwood Scrubs. The escort was in command of a former London policeman who welcomed the assignment as he wanted to visit his wife. My brother Leslie, who had joined the Scots Guards, had already been in France, fought in the battle of Mons, been blown up by a 'Jack Johnston', had recovered and was back in barracks in London. Before going for the train I took my escort home where my mother gave us a good supper. I had to advise my brother when we would arrive in London and he got leave and came to meet us. The escort were quite willing that he should take charge of me for the day and we arranged to meet at the gates of Wormwood Scrubs late in the afternoon and the escort went off to visit friends. I am sure my brother was more affected seeing me disappear behind the gates of prison than he had been by his war experiences.

There is nothing romantic about prison. At best it is a miserable and humiliating experience. Wormwood Scrubs had been greatly improved as the result of the suffragette prisoners, many of whom were influential. They had exposed the conditions in their day. Walls were painted in two colours. I only appreciated how important this was after I was sent to the Calton prison in Edinburgh where everything was in a deadening whitewash. The real punishment of prison, as was explained to me later by famous prison authority Dr Devon, the head of Scottish Prisons,[5] is that it cuts a person off from his friends and normal life. It also to some extent cuts them off from other human beings so far as speaking is concerned. To a person who is suddenly transferred from a bustling activity in the outer world to the deadly torture of confinement the shock can be quite shattering.

From time to time, especially in the Calton, one heard outbreaks of shouting when the nerves of some prisoner had cracked. There were many serving soldiers and sailors who came to prison and found the silence and loneliness more than they could stand. They had to go to the padded cell in case they hurt themselves. That prisons have padded cells I can testify for on one occasion, to make room for a mission service, I was temporarily parked in one. After a time the COs were advised of these effects of prison and in any case I had been a reader of Jack London who gave his readers advice on how to deal with such situations. So when I was being registered and I was given the Bible and the *Pilgrim's Progress* I asked if I might have educational books as well. The shock of a prisoner asking for educational books shook the warder. He gave me a curious look and asked if I had been there before. He thought I knew the ropes. So I did, thanks to Jack London! Any normal criminal asking for educational books would have got all he wanted. But this was a luxury for a CO so the answer was 'No'!

Workshop activity in prison helps to lighten the misery – one at least sees other faces – but I was never allowed outside my cell. As this continued in later imprisonments, I think I must have spent more time in solitary confinement than most people involved in the struggle. COs in prison were in general treated worse than criminals. In the case of criminals, the warders did their job without personal feelings, but in the case of COs, they had the normal resentments of the general public and felt it was their duty to impose the full rigours of the law. At first one tried to count the time. Taking a step as a second and the length of the cell six steps, ten times made a minute and six hundred times an hour and so on. This one soon realised was a maddening pastime. But the windows were too high to see out of, there was nothing to see or

---

[5]   James Devon (1866–1939), prison medical officer and criminologist, author of *Some Causes of Crime* (1908) and *The Criminal in the Community* (1912) and medical commissioner to the Scottish Prison Commission 1913–29.

do, and it was almost impossible to acclimatise oneself to this life of a cabbage – it at least sees the sun.

I have one outstandingly pleasant memory of Wormwood Scrubs. In the silence of one Sunday night in winter, we suddenly heard a beautiful contralto voice coming up from the grounds outside singing 'England Arise'. I have seldom been so moved and I am sure we all felt we were not entirely forgotten. I think these fifty-six days were the longest in my life. In due course another escort arrived to take me back to Glencorse Barracks. My escort, as before when we were passing through Edinburgh, took me home to see my mother who of course was not very happy at my lot but never by word or look did she show disapproval or say anything to distress me.

My return to Glencorse created almost consternation. I was the first CO to come back. Normally COs had had their first court martial and on arrival at prison they were interviewed and after some time were sent to work centres, timber felling, road making or other national work. This did not happen to me and I can only guess that Major Robertson's illusion that I was the 'brains' of war resistance had followed me. At any rate, Glencorse resented my being handed to them again and they hurriedly got rid of me by a second court martial and a further sentence of one year. So once more I was escorted to Wormwood Scrubs. On arrival my escort was told that new regulations were in force and that we were to go [to] our nearest local prison. The escort wanted to have the day in London and after some enquiries as to how they could have me kept in custody, they took me to the Tower of London. Here I became for a short time a 'prisoner in the Tower'.

[How many good honest men and women have entered there as prisoners, how many have never left it, how many left to provide fuel for the bonfire of a crowd thirsting for the blood or torture of victims, whose sole offence was daring to hold a different opinion. Picture Sir Thomas More embraced by his favourite daughter on his way up Tower Hill to his pedestal. Picture proud Northumberland, who renounced his faith on the bloody platform on the promise of a pardon at the last moment, but 'put not your faith in princes nor men's sons' – that pledge was broken and he lost his head with honour. Here also Sir Walter Raleigh paid the penalty of daring to marry the woman he loved and got his reward for his patriotism. And the list of those who never left, victims of that monster Henry VIII and his daughters – what a history of murder, vice, and crime. It seems so ridiculous that a man or woman should be put on such an absolute pedestal, and all the remainder bow, beg, and obey his every whim, murder each other by the orders of or for the favour of this deity. Elizabeth insisted on everyone round living the unnatural life she chose for herself. There seems to me something entirely stupid in this excessive servility and surrender of all moral control, to any villain or imbecile who happened to arrive on this pedestal.

Some were indeed men, but I confess, I admire those religious martyrs – fanatics if you will – who could look on anyone of them from queen downwards and say I am a man, and will be servile to none, bowing only to God. From that attitude and from these men has sprung liberty, liberty of thought, conscience, speech and press. They paid [for] it with their blood on the scaffold, in the throes of torture, on the gibbet, and in the dungeons. The history of liberty lies in those channels, and not in the catalogue of feudal murders, and from time to time mutual extermination.

From the earliest history, this war element has been mostly occasioned by lust. Our country raided by Saxons and Angles and other teutonic tribes – actuated by lust of plunder ... Then we have William the Conqueror collecting all the thieves and rogues of the continent to whom he promises fat hauls, and overrunning this country. Lord Lytton says it was immaterial to the most of the population who were their masters, hence his success. Curiously enough, people pride themselves on being of Norman descent. It seems to me almost equivalent to an Australian claiming boastfully descent from some of the convict settlers who were many of them better men than the Norman brigands. Some of these spread to Scotland, amongst whom we have the great great grandfathers of Sir William Wallace, Robert the Bruce, Comyn Baliol etc.

Some of these had managed to secure in the divide land both in England and Scotland in both of which countries the rogues continually quarrelled over the spoil, especially where the chief of the brigands' power was tapered off towards the north of England. Needless to say, a slave was still a slave. Some, of course, wished to set up business on their own account. And after David was successful in squashing the Celts a fairly secure king business was established in Norman hands. The chief Norman robber down south was threatened and almost toppled by the new start, and but for the Galloway men's conceit and a mere chance, most of England might have called itself Scotland.

Later on Scotland was nearly becoming England, and then we have the Norman knight Sir William Wallace resenting the southern Normans touching his property, and like ancient Redmonds and Carsons began to show their tools how their homes and properties were in danger etc. and of course more bloodshed for 'Scottish Independence' which meant that the local Normans were not to be usurped by the other Normans.

Then after another Norman comes from the English court to buy and set up in this Scottish kingship; and they adopt a fairly sensible means of settling their differences – they call in arbitration, the loser will not accept the decision, commits a murder or two, starts on his own and gradually gains a following sufficient to establish him in business. Then we have Bannockburn where 'Scottish Independence' was won.

About this time in England, or a little earlier, more than half the population were slaves or serfs. Scotland would probably be worse and many reigns afterwards the largest part of the population were mendicants. When Edward I held Scotland, the peasants were free to cultivate a little peace although their fields and crops were liable to be trodden down by any 'hero' in a tin suit that chose to pass, but this little period of English rule, so far as the economic condition of the productive classes was concerned, is marked by some little betterment. The success of Bruce, which was partly due to ... the pit spikes etc. and was supposed to be adopted from the advice of some foreigner who had seen such a plan in Spain or somewhere, set all the local iron-clads again clattering, to the misery of all in their path.

Dickens pictures the establisher of 'one of our old Norman families' clad in steel from head to toe, mounted on an armour clad horse, courageously leading forward his soldiers clad in leathern jerkins. Needless to say the iron-clad was usually in more danger from his armour than his foe.

Just picture the economic conditions of the few people who were not slaves, and then think of these peoples following Bruce, Baliol or Edward who were all Norman-English, and picture where the difference in independence would arise. If it was not love of independence (which people would have us believe these serfs enjoyed) what would prompt them to take sides with Bruce against the English? The same as prompted in later days the clans to take the side opposite to the well off and opulent. If these early feudal slaves had no vision of liberty, they had visions of the amount of spoil that would remain on the field by a beaten English-Norman army. Fine armour, horses, supplies of all kinds. Needed those starving and poor wretches any further inducement? No doubt they would also have a good deal of 'terrible times they would have to endure under the enemy when victorious etc.', but that is not 'national feeling'. All the fighting up to the end of the eighteenth century had stealing and counter-stealing as its inspiring farce [*sic*].

The people at the reformation and other revolutions who were sincere were perhaps in all classes, but the majority of the persecutions, bloodshed, martyrdom, etc. were the result of the advantage being taken by the social vultures to rob and plunder. Thus when sincere men wished to rid the RC [Roman Catholic] Church of its vice and malpractices while leaving what was good in it, all sorts of people took sides and made this the excuse for transfer of property to themselves. To cover this, persecution, torture, mobs excited to arson and destruction, and all imaginable was instituted. And since our Protestant party was victorious they wrote the history and thus we have the picture of their side as angelic.

We must continuously keep this in mind when reading history. It was mostly written by the ultimately victorious party and nearly all contrary views suppressed. Disraeli says it would require a man of exceptional courage to re-write history true. He gives examples of men at the beginning of the nineteenth century no one sees mentioned in history, but who were more accountable for the happenings at that time than the accepted stars. Read his view of Pitt and compare it with what is taught in schools. W. Cobbett wrote a book about the Reformation in England[6] just to shock the satisfied righteousness of our justice and the continual 'holy' manner in which we deal with every other opinion. Cobbett's book was translated by the RCs into many languages as their view. Apply all this to the present day. Since 1789 people have commenced to fight for liberty. Some liberty has been gained. The colliers and salt workers in Scotland actually became free from serfdom about 1799 – a little over one hundred years ago.

For making speeches asking [for] manhood suffrage etc., people were sent to plantations and some hanged. We have the martyrs at the time of the Reform Bill, those who went to prison for the freedom of the press – Cobbett about the last, for twelve months – for freedom of speech. The Chartists and the starving populace who dared to ask for food were robbed and shot by those who were making this country 'honoured and respected abroad'. Were the continental wars winning liberty for the people here? Or was it gained by these persecuted men? The last of those martyrs for freedom to be secured in the Tower of London, I think, were the Chartists – whose policy is still being demanded by democracy.

These thoughts were perhaps wrapped in that haze which envelops one on entering a place where mystery and grimness seem to combine, but it seemed to me that history as written there would be incomplete without some connection between that fortress and the most noteworthy persecution of conscience of modern times, but at least one representative of those who stand for liberty of thought was led and imprisoned there.]

---

[6]   William Cobbett, *History of the Protestant Reformation* (London, 1824–7).

The guard room where I was deposited had a motley collection of soldiers. One had come from Wandsworth where he had already spent a year and he related the terrible things he had seen done to the COs. About twenty Irish soldiers who had overstayed their leave and were on the way back to the front under escort were interested to know if this was true and I could verify that such incidents were taking place. This soldier from Wandsworth then turned his attention to me. He appeared a typical musical comedy type of Frenchman, which he turned out to be. He had a musical and pleasant voice and spoke with earnest eloquence. He was in a dreadful state of apprehension. The soldiers at Wandsworth had not only alarmed him about the treatment of COs but they created panic by their prophesies about his own fate. He thought he could get some reassurance from me, I suppose. His story was a strange one. He claimed to be the son of a French marquis – the marquis de Beauregard – and a noble lady of France to whom he was not married. He was born about the time of the Franco Prussian war of 1870–1 and at the time of the siege of Paris, the parents brought the child to Edinburgh for reasons of discretion and safety and they left him to be brought up by a baker and his wife at Elm Row. He could not have known that I knew Edinburgh and could therefore check all his references. He remained there till he had finished his schooling when his father came to decide what career he was to follow. Naturally, from his upbringing he wanted to be a baker. His father agreed and took him back to Paris to be trained by one of the best chefs in Paris.

When he had completed his training he was brought to London to make his own way in life. His mother had long since got married to some other man and there was no home for him in France. He made a successful career for himself and at the beginning of the war he was chef to a member of the Rothschild family. When his employer went into the army he took his chef with him. Here he was the prince of chefs, catering for his master and his fellow officers, with a well-equipped kitchen and staff under his orders. Alas for him, according to his story, an army order was issued that all personnel in barracks were to be enlisted men and he was compelled to join the army. From being the boss in the kitchen he suddenly found himself taking orders from non-commissioned officers who had previously been bossed by him, and who in his view were much inferior to himself.

In his rage and frustration, he had been airing his grievances spiced with much abuse of the British army and Britain. He was tipped off that his remarks had been overheard and written down and that he was going to be in serious trouble. He took panic and, with another soldier, deserted and took off for London. For some time they lived on their wits. They found lodgings near a hospital and pretended they were employed there. He lived by writing 'touching' letters to the many Rothschild guests who had appreciated his cooking. All was going well till a chance visitor learned from the landlady of her lodgers from the hospital and told her there were no such people there. The landlady, reflecting on his foreign look and accent, concluded that he must be a spy and notified the police. They were both arrested and sentenced to twelve months for obtaining money under false pretences.

While he was in prison, lawyers arrived to tell him his father had died and left him a large sum of money and he returned to his cell to finish his sentence. When the time came for them to be released, his regiment wanted nothing more to do with him. His partner was returned to the army but he had been rearrested and brought to the Tower. The soldiers there had terrified him by telling him he was to be tried as a spy. I had no means of knowing what happened to him in the end.

This all came back to me nearly fifty years later when I was given a book to read by the librarian of the House of Commons which dealt with the life of the Victorians and their 'morality'. It was called *The Girl with the Swansdown Seat* by Cyril Pearl,[7] published by Frederick Miller, London, 1955. It makes the modern 'permissive age' appear almost puritanical and the role – one might almost say 'rule' – of the prostitute in upper-class society gives some idea of the profligacy and provocative extravagance of the nobility and the rich. For example, the *Edinburgh Review* in 1859 said when one walked down certain streets in Edinburgh, Glasgow and London, 'the stones seemed alive with lust'. It was estimated that the whores of London had 2,000,000 clients a week. The most outrageous extravagance quoted is the £40,000 paid by Lord Hertford for one night's entertainment which his Lordship made so exacting that the lady had to spend the next three days in bed. Amongst these notorious much sought after ladies was a miss Howard, who already had amassed a considerable fortune at the age of seventeen when in 1839 she met Louis Napoleon, then rather down on his luck in London. At that time her clients included the duke of Beaufort, the earl of Malmesbury, Lord Chesterfield and the count d'Orsay. Already at 17 she was a wealthy girl and 'able to lay at the exiles' feet her strong box as well as her heart'. (She is said to have been paid £1,000 by Lord Clebden for one single demonstration of her skill!) Elizabeth Howard provided the money for Louis Napoleon's campaign to capture the throne of France and eventually, when he succeeded in 1848 in being

---

[7]   Cyril Altson Pearl (1904–1987), Australian journalist, biographer and social historian. *The Girl with the Swansdown Seat* was his revisionist study of Victorian sexual morality.

elected President, Elizabeth Howard became his Consort. (He had been imprisoned for six years after his first attempt from which he escaped.) In 1851 he became dictator and Emperor of France. He now desired to found a royal line and Elizabeth was not a suitable candidate. She was pensioned off with £20,000 a year and a sum of about £250,000 and an estate of about 450 acres near Versailles. She was made the countess of Beauregard and her son by a previous lover was made the count de Bechevet. She had failed to produce a son for Louis. I have not been able to trace the connection if any between this Beauregard family and my acquaintance of the Tower but Louis' downfall in 1871 would certainly fit in with the dates of a Beauregard flight from Paris. It was interesting to read that Elizabeth Howard later married Clarence Trelawney and they came to Ross-shire for two years.

In the evening, when I was due to be collected by my escort to catch the Edinburgh train, the regimental sergeant major of the military police, who seemed to be responsible for the discipline of the whole London area, came to collect me from the guard room. He took me round a bit of the Tower and let me see 'the ceremony of the keys' which precedes the closing of the Tower for the night. He had a long discussion with me about the war and its causes and parted with me with good wishes and a friendly handshake when my escort arrived. My destination was the Calton Jail in Edinburgh which was situated on Regent Road on the site to be later covered by St Andrews House which I was to occupy again thirty years later as Secretary of State for Scotland.

Wormwood Scrubs could not in any way be described as a happy abode but on entering the Calton Jail I felt the cold chill of a grim fortress – a 'Colditz in Edinburgh'. It was what it looked. Neither in its decor nor its amenities had it had the reforming benefits of suffrage education. Its walls were deadly white and there was no colour to be seen. This seems a trifle but many months later when being taken to do a job, I had to pass a courtyard with green grass growing [and] I was nearly moved to tears. In Wormwood Scrubs the walls were painted with warm colours and the Chapel made one forget it was in a prison.

The Calton seemed the poorhouse of all prisons. My first meal of two pints of broth and and twelve oz dry bread was in harmony with the surroundings. The meals consisted of, for breakfast, six oz of oatmeal steamed into porridge, and half a pint butter milk; for midday meal, two pints of broth and twelve oz dry bread, and for supper, eight oz oatmeal steamed into porridge with three-quarters of a pint of butter milk. The 'bed' was three planks of highly polished wood made to form a board six and a half feet long and two feet broad. It folded down from the wall and the covering was a sheet and one pillow, which slipped off the board from time to time during the night and wakened the prisoner with his head bumping down on the bare boards. In winter there were three blankets of what seemed the thinnest material available. No mattress was provided for the first month and I was physically insufficiently upholstered in these days to avoid the pain of supporting myself on these boards by what seemed a sharp point on my pelvis bone.

The first cell I was put in – a 'reception cell' – was dark with large bare pipes exposed. I had placed the stool so that I could sit with my back to the wall for support. When the warder opened the door at two o'clock, he asked immediately:

'Whit are ye daeing sitting with your back to that wall getting yer claes a' white?'

I replied, 'I did not know it would come off'.

'Whit made ye think it wadna come off?' he continued.

'I took for granted it would be sized', I explained

'Ye had nae business to think', I was told.

I was then taken to the official reception. It went as follows:

'Where dae ye come from?'

'Glencorse!'

'Its a dawm peety they didna shoot you at Glencorse!'

'Well I dare say that would save me some trouble too'

'I ken what I wad dae wi' you!'

'I can assure you that it is no desire of mine that I am troubling you with a visit!'

'Weel, take a bath if that will not interfere with your conscience!'

In Scotland a prisoner was supplied only with a Bible and hymn book compared with Bible, hymn book, *Pilgrim's Progress*, dictionary and slate, which was the issue in Wormwood Scrubs. In the Scrubs the doctor made a careful examination to decide what job was suitable for the prisoner. In Edinburgh one got a dab on the chest with a stethoscope and the decision 'all right'. I suppose this is all right in the majority of cases but a mistake might be made. Hot air was supposed to be blown into my cell but, as might be expected in these inhospitable surroundings, in my case it was cold and eventually I had to be whipped off to hospital for a month. My blood was evidently turning to water. My diet was sweet milk and bread. Nothing I think has ever tasted to me more wonderful.

After serving four months of my sentence I was suddenly released and taken back to Glencorse. There was no explanation either to me or to the Barracks and after holding me in custody for some weeks they decided to get rid of me by another court martial. They sent me back to finish my year's sentence. At the end of the period I went back again to Glencorse. This time they had word of some change of policy towards COs and I was kept for some time till they received official instructions. However they were embarrassed by my presence which, as can be understood, upset the good order of their routine work. So they gave me a short sentence to give time for the new regulations to come through. When nothing happened during this period and I came back once more, they decided it was no good trying to understand government policy and they gave me another court martial to get rid of me for good. This time I was sentenced to two years. I had five DCMs (district court martials) as they were called and I said goodbye to Glencorse. I was an awful nuisance to the people there who were made to do what they found disagreeable and unpleasant. Their friendly treatment and their endeavours to mix justice with consideration curiously enough made it more difficult to stand aside, but we both had to do what we regarded as our duty in the circumstances. It is difficult after fifty years to explain one's attitude but there is no doubt that the protest made changed the mind of the people about the then causes of war and the old idea expressed by Foch[8] that spheres of trade are cleared by cannon shot made way for efforts to find ways of settling international disputes by other and less violent means.

In a discussion with Dr Devon, the chairman of the Prison Commission in Scotland, when he came to persuade us to give up a hunger strike, he explained that in his view, prison was not meant to inflict physical punishment on prisoners but to separate them from their friends and outside amenities. Prisoners were therefore given work to do. The main activities in Scotland were the sewing of mailbags and the plaiting of coir mats. Both had disastrous effects on soft hands. It was easy by a slip of the needle to end up with a poisoned finger. There were work facilities in common with other prisoners but I had practically solitary confinement from start to finish. This has a very depressing effect and not everyone survives without harm.

James McDougall,[9] who had been arrested with James Maxton[10] on Glasgow Green, for example, went berserk and had to be removed

[8]   Marshal Ferdinand Jean Marie Foch (1851–1929), French military theorist and commander.
[9]   James Dunlop MacDougall (1891–1963), socialist activist and politician, arrested with James Maxton on 29 March 1916 and convicted in the High Court of Justiciary in Edinburgh in May. He was transferred from Calton Jail to Perth Prison Hospital in August to serve out the rest of his sentence. He joined the Communist Party of Great Britain in the early 1920s but moved towards both Liberal and Conservative politics thereafter.
[10] James Maxton (1885–1946), socialist activist and politician, Chairman of the ILP 1913–19 and prominent MP for Glasgow Bridgeton from 1922 until his death. Led ILP disaffiliation from the Labour Party in 1932.

shouting and roaring, having cracked under the strain. This happened with sailors from Scapa Flow and others from time to time. We had one hour's exercise a day in the prison yard. The routine was for the prisoners to march round two rings, each prisoner maintaining a gap of about six feet from the one in front. Communication by speech or otherwise was forbidden but we developed the art of whispering when far enough away from the supervising warders. The exercise provided the opportunity for prisoners to visit the toilets. If we were not immediately in front of a friend the idea was to drop out for toilet purposes and then return to the ring. The warder waited till he saw a large gap between two prisoners and the waiting prisoner was then signed to enter the ring. So when we saw one of our friends waiting we slowed down and made a large gap at the appropriate point and the waiting friend came in behind and we were able to talk. I became quite expert at this game and at speaking without moving my lips which was what the warder watched for. It took me long to recover the normal use of my lips when speaking. When tired I can still lapse into the ventriloquist's immobility.

The most welcome facility was the library. A warder and prisoner came round once a week with a trolley of books and the man in the cell could take his pick. As my speed of reading soon exhausted an ordinary book and the only hope was to take some difficult reading to slow me up, I asked if there were any books in French, German or Spanish. I discovered there was a Cassells' Self Educator[11] which had nearly every subject. There were eight volumes and they became my standby during the whole period of my stay. I doubt if any other subscriber ever read the books so thoroughly as I did and I learned a great deal on every subject from art to do-it-yourself activities. On the literature side, I owe an eternal debt of gratitude to Sir Walter Scott. I found his novels difficult to read when at school but I now read all his books with deep interest. I found his prefaces especially rewarding. However, this solves the problem of prison for a mere fraction of the time and prison would still be prison if it were in the British Museum.

I mentioned 'friends' in prison. There were a number of COs there who were opposing the war for varied reasons. One from Dundee described himself simply as a Christian and refused to comply with any rules which he considered were made for criminals. On entering prison he was asked what his religion was. He replied 'Christian'! The warder looked down the list he had – Presbyterian, Catholic, English Church, Unitarian, etc. – and said to Barclay, 'We have nothing of that kind here, I'll put you down as a Presbyterian'. Another character was

---

[11] *Cassell's Popular Educator* (8 vols, London, 1900).

Robert Stewart,[12] a member of Scrymgeour's socialist Prohibition Party in Dundee. When he was asked his religion he replied 'none'. The reply was that there was no category in prison for anyone without a religion and he was put down as a Quaker. This led to some confusion. The chaplain, an elderly man choke full of every establishment prejudice, went into Stewart's cell and jauntily greeted him 'I see you are a Quaker'. 'You see wrong, then,' replied Stewart. When Bob Stewart finally explained to him that he was an atheist, the chaplain nearly dropped with shock. It was the first time he had experienced an atheist in prison and he felt this was in some way a disgrace to the congregation. For some time his sermons to all the prisoners were directed to Stewart and I am sure few of the prisoners knew what he was talking about.

When the war ended, some concessions were granted to political prisoners. We were allowed books in and among others, I asked for the works of Bernard Shaw which I had received in a present during my absence from a brother. The chaplain refused permission and declared that if he had his way they would all be burned. Later, I learned that a Welsh trade unionist, Stanley Rees, had been able to get Marx's *Capital* in three volumes and, of course, I immediately made an application. This was granted. The chaplain on his next visit explained to me that he had studied economics himself at the university and he had looked through Marx's economics and could find nothing about socialism in them. But Shaw! Barclay refused to obey any prison rules. He explained to the governor that these did not apply to him since he was not a criminal. So he spent a great deal of his time in the punishment cells on bread and water. We saw him going from a burly joiner, as I think he was, to a knock-kneed old man with a long beard like Methuselah. He was ingenious. The windows were covered with lamp black to black out the light against air raids. Barclay used to rub the toilet paper on the windows and manufacture his own carbon paper. He then used some hard point to write long screeds from Revelations and other parts of the Bible and pass them surreptitiously to other prisoners. It was in this way we learned about his various punishments.

The best known of my fellow prisoners was, of course, James Maxton. He personified and led the ILP for many years. He anticipated later fashions by keeping his black hair long which with

---

[12]   Robert J. Stewart (1877-1971), organiser of the Scottish Prohibition Party established as a breakaway from the ILP in 1904 by Edwin Scrymgeour (1866-1947), independent socialist, prohibitionist and MP for Dundee 1922-31. Stewart established the rival National Prohibition and Reform Party before the First World War and, when war broke out, was an organiser for the No Conscription Fellowship. After the war Stewart became a prominent founding member of the Communist Party of Great Britain.

his black eyebrows and long face made him a political Hamlet. He was one of the most effective and charming propagandists of the socialist movement. He was a teacher and at the Glasgow University he had actually been chairman of the Conservative group of students at the time Walter Elliot,[13] a later Tory Minister, was a Fabian. Maxton was more a prophet than a practical politician. He had been arrested at a meeting in Glasgow Green and sentenced to one year for sedition. Another two were involved – James MacDougall, another teacher, and Jack Smith,[14] who had been in the chair.

It was the week after the Easter Rising in Ireland in 1916. There had been a social and dance and I was through from Edinburgh in company with Barbara Halliday,[15] who was later to become my wife, and her brother. At the dance a young man who had come from Ireland had copies of the *Irish Republican* for the last three weeks. One described some of the events the week before the rising, the second was the week of the rising, and the last was the week after. I got one of the copies which I regarded as a historical document. Jack Smith got the second and my future brother-in-law got the third. Jack Smith had this paper in his pocket when he was arrested at the meeting the following day and when the judge passed sentence, although he had only been the chairman and had not made any seditious speech, Maxton and MacDougall got twelve months and Jack Smith got eighteen months for having this paper in his pocket.

Maxton was, even in prison, the warder's pet among the prisoners. He was given a job in a little carpentry shop in the tower from which he could see all the movements of the trains in the Waverley Station – and only those who have experienced solitary confinement can appreciate what a privilege it was to have a window on life. The warders used to go in and talk with him which also helped to break the time.

---

[13] Walter Elliot (1888–1958), Unionist politician and MP for Lanark (1918–23), Glasgow Kelvingrove (1924–45, 1950–8), Scottish Universities (1946–50).

[14] Jack Smith, anarchist shop steward at Weir's munitions factory.

[15] Barbara Woodburn [*née* Halliday], teacher, Labour activist and politician. She was an honorary lecturer in the Labour College and active within the Edinburgh Trades and Labour Council, sitting on the executive and acting as its representative on the board of the Edinburgh Royal Infirmary. She contested Edinburgh South in the parliamentary election of 1935 and contested a number of Edinburgh seats in municipal elections before being elected for Central Leith in October 1937.

Another well-known prisoner was Willie Gallacher,[16] the leader of the Clyde Workers' Committee, who with John Muir,[17] the Secretary, had been sentenced earlier for an article in the *Worker*. The origin of this paper was the suppression of the *Forward*, the paper founded and run by Tom Johnston, who later became Secretary of State for Scotland. The Clyde Workers' Committee had called a mass strike of munitions workers to protest against the eviction of families of soldiers to make room for immigrant munition workers who, with their high wages, were able to pay higher rents. There was a further demand that profiteering should be curbed. As a result of this, Lloyd George, who was Minister of Munitions, had the 'Munitions Act' passed which restricted profits.

To calm the situation he came and held a meeting in Glasgow. The main newspapers had been warned not to report the meeting. David Kirkwood,[18] later the MP for Dumbarton Burghs, was in the chair and in the event, in addition to the lecture to munition workers by Lloyd George, there was a lecture to Lloyd George by Kirkwood on behalf of the men. The *Forward* reported the meeting under the heading 'Best paid munition worker visits the Clyde. £5000 a year'. Lloyd George was furious and shortly after the *Forward* was suppressed. When challenged in Parliament by Tom Johnston[19] he denied there

[16]   William Gallacher (1881–1965), activist and politician, MP for West Fife 1935–50. A member of the British Socialist Party and a shop steward at the Albion Works, he became chairman of the Clyde Workers' Committee (CWC) and in April 1916 was imprisoned with Muir for twelve months for publishing an article, 'Should the workers arm?', in the Committee's journal, *The Worker*. It was the first of four stints as a political prisoner. He played a prominent role in the establishment of the Communist Party of Great Britain (CPGB) in 1920 and served on its central committee from 1921 until 1963, and became its honorary president in 1956.

[17]   John William Muir (1879–1931), activist and politician, MP for Glasgow Maryhill 1922–4. A member of the Socialist Labour Party and a skilled worker at Barr and Stroud engineering works, he was a prominent member of the CWC and presented its plans to Lloyd George at the December 1915 meeting. He was imprisoned with Gallacher.

[18]   David Kirkwood, first Baron Kirkwood (1872–1955), trade unionist and politician, MP for Dumbarton Burghs 1922–50 and East Dunbartonshire 1950–1. Member of the Socialist Labour Party and, from 1914, the ILP, Kirkwood was a shop steward at Parkhead Forge and played a major role in the industrial militancy of the First World War. He was deported to Edinburgh in March 1916.

[19]   Thomas Johnston (1881–1965), journalist, politician, MP for West Stirlingshire 1922–4, 1929–31, 1935–45 and Dundee 1924–9. A member of the ILP, Johnston began his career in municipal government in Kirkintilloch and established the weekly paper, *The Forward*, in 1906, which he edited until 1933. He was Under-secretary of state for Scotland in 1929–31, briefly Lord Privy Seal in 1931 and Secretary of State for Scotland 1941–5. AW here probably conflates Lloyd George's tortuous parliamentary defence of the suppression in 1916 and subsequent parliamentary attacks on the episode, such as David Kirkwood's in *Parliamentary Debates* (Commons), 23 November 1922, cols 132–8.

was any connection between the suppression and the article but no one believed this. However, he was taken at his word and a new paper was produced, the *Worker*, and the first issue was confined to a reprint of the offending report of the meeting. Within weeks, the editor, John Muir, later MP for Maryhill, and Willie Gallacher, the chairman, were arrested and sentenced for, I think, a year. The article on which the charge was based was headed 'Should the workers arm' and the question was answered in the negative. It was said that the later Rt Hon. John Wheatley,[20] Ramsay MacDonald's great Minister of Housing, had written the article but the *Worker* was duly punished.

This collection in the Calton Jail made, therefore, a goodly company and we all knew each other as well as having common interests. The only time we met 'socially' was in the bible class. There was a friendly missionary who held a bible class on the Sunday afternoons and during this period it must have been a unique gathering. Knowing the torture of the silence rule on prisoners, he had devised a way of letting us hear our voices. He invited us to quote texts from the Bible and this sent us all to search for quotations that said what we wanted to say. By the time we got there, Jack Smith was reciting poems and as these were in tune with the proceedings, no exception was taken. It became a different matter when Bob Stewart produced his poem which he had written – a violent diatribe about war which he declaimed with passion. The missionary thought we might confine ourselves to the Bible in future. If he did not know before, he soon discovered that the Bible itself could be used as a revolutionist's handbook. I can almost hear now Bob Stewart declaiming:

> Woe unto you, scribes and Pharisees, hypocrites! for ye devour widows' houses and for a pretence make long prayers therefore ye shall receive the greater damnation. Woe unto you, scribes and Pharisees, hypocrites! for ye compass sea and land to make one proselyte, and when he is made, ye make him twofold more the child of hell than yourselves.[21]

The quotations had to come to an end when a sailor who had read Shelley's[22] prose works, which were in the library, quoted some of the

---

[20] John Wheatley (1869-1930), politician and publisher, MP for Glasgow Shettleston 1922-30. A member of the ILP, Wheatley was a driving force in Glasgow municipal politics and closely involved with the CWC. He was Minister for Health in the 1924 Labour government and his Housing (Financial Provisions) Act was its sole substantial legislative achievement.

[21] Matthew 23:14–15.

[22] Percy Bysshe Shelley (1792–1822), poet whose work inspired radicals of all shades.

lurid bible extracts which Shelley had used to shock his readers. The little missionary hardly deserved this for his efforts to brighten the lives of prisoners. I received occasional news of what was happening outside from the Unitarian minister who visited the Calton. He was a personal friend and sympathetic. Nevertheless, we felt as if we were marooned on some inaccessible island.

So imagination played a large part in our thinking. When I was returned to the Calton just before Christmas 1916, there had been headlines on the posters that peace approaches had been made by the Kaiser. So on Christmas night, when I heard what appeared to be church bells pealing, it was easy to imagine that peace had come. Alas! after a time I came to the conclusion that it was workmen clanging the tramrails in the street outside.

CHAPTER THREE

One of my recreations before the war had been singing. I sang in choirs both church and secular. I also was in some demand for concerts which were then a feature of social life. Only once did I sing professionally. I was engaged to sing after a dinner in one of the fashionable restaurants. Once was enough. By the time the concert part started one could hardly see the diners for smoke and I concluded that no fee could compensate for such an experience.

However my singing brought some interesting experiences. At the outbreak of the war, the then Prime Minister, Mr Asquith,[1] spoke in the Usher Hall on the war. The Edinburgh Choral Union and Mooney's Choir, of which I was a member, were asked to provide musical inspiration. It was an opportunity to hear the Prime Minister. I felt he was not very convincing and was rather disappointed. But the meeting provided the most dramatic scene I have ever witnessed at a public meeting. Lord Rosebery,[2] a former Prime Minister, had been invited to speak at the meeting and had refused. I had heard him speak in the same hall and deliver a violent attack on Asquith and Lloyd George for their attack on the Lords. I could appreciate that it was probably true that he had never forgiven Asquith. It was also said he would not play second fiddle to Asquith.

Asquith after his speech left to go to another meeting and was followed by J. Avon Clyde,[3] the Lord Advocate. He had just ended his supporting speech when Rosebery was seen to rise from his seat at the front corner of the grand tier and move up the stairs as if to leave the hall. A shout went up from the audience: 'Rosebery!' He turned half way up the steps and turned like one of the aristocrats on the steps of

---

[1] Herbert Henry Asquith (1852–1928), politician, Home Secretary 1892–5, Chancellor of the Exchequer 1905–8 and Prime Minister 1908–16.
[2] Archibald Philip Primrose, fifth earl of Rosebery and first earl of Midlothian (1847–1929), politician and writer, Prime Minister 1894–5.
[3] James Avon Clyde, Lord Clyde (1863–1944), judge and politician, Lord Advocate 1916–20.

the guillotine and ceremoniously bowed. With his white silky hair and white scarf thrown round his neck, no actor could have played the part more effectively. The crowd then called 'Speech! Speech!' and viewed from the platform, we saw the thousand people in the seats sway to one side just as if it had been a field of yellow corn bent by the wind. Lord Rosebery then slowly descended the steps, grasped the rail at the corner of the grand tier with a gesture of resolution and declaimed, 'Well, Gentlemen, I will!' Then followed an oration which I am sure had been carefully prepared and he completely captured the meeting.

My singing involved me in other incidents. I was asked to sing at the annual social of the newsvendors' mission in the Grassmarket. In the interval prizes were presented for the winners on their sports outing. The winning football team were asked to stand and instead of the usual eleven, twenty-two stood up and the dispute as to who had won developed into a free fight. One very belligerent young man, tall and handsome except for a lost eye, sat just in front of us and was evidently going to join in when a powerful man beside him pinioned his arms to the back of the seat. I mention this because during my stay in the Calton Jail, this man came there after having been sentenced to death for having murdered his mistress. He had thrown her out of the window in Jamaica Street in north Edinburgh.[4] The day he was hanged, a strange silence settled over the prison and all the prisoners were confined to their cells till the ceremony was over. For some time, towards the end of the war, the COs were no longer exercised with criminals but in a small yard apart and it was a strange experience to walk round what was evidently the graveyard for the murderers who had been executed in the Calton. Murray's tablet was there!

When I became a member of the ILP, which was a very social organisation, I was roped in to sing at their concerts and social evenings. A singing friend of mine was invited to sing at one such gathering and was asked to visit the home of the accompanist for a rehearsal of his songs. He felt he needed some support in meeting this unknown lady and insisted that I should accompany him. The young lady turned out to be a teacher whose father and brothers were members of the ILP. She herself was also a fine contralto as well as a pianist. She was a picture in her black velvet dress against her marble-smooth and finely moulded features. The evening developed into a party and we sang for the rest of the night. We also discussed politics and drama and I needed little persuasion to join the group and go to the dance. I was

---

[4]   AW seems to have confused his memories here. The trial of Philip Murray, the one-eyed newsvendor, occurred in 1923 and he was convicted for the murder of William Cree. A considerable crowd gathered on Calton Hill on the morning of his execution, *Scotsman*, 9 and 31 October 1923.

delighted to meet someone with whom one could discuss ideas as well as music, opera and theatre, and as I had already booked two seats for the opera at the end of the week, the acceptance of my invitation to join me promised me more charming company than I had hoped for. As might be imagined, the friendship grew and as we were all attending the many meetings being held at this time, Barbara Halliday and I became constant companions.

As controversy developed over the war, all those who opposed it tended to come together. Her home had been one of those that gave hospitality to visiting speakers and Maxton and other ILP speakers from the west of Scotland were regular visitors. Life became one long discussion and argument about the war and when we joined the anti-conscription movement we met a great variety of interesting people. I had not realised that there were so many varieties of socialist thought. The Labour Party at that time was a federation of several organisations. The Fabians and the ILP were the idea-forming and evangelical elements and the trades unions provided the mass.

Outside this Labour Party group there were the Social Democratic Federation which was the strongest of the groups who claimed to be followers of Karl Marx. One of their members in Edinburgh was the minister of Old Greyfriars,[5] the church of the Covenanters. This minister used to lecture us after the service on socialism and other moralities. There was the Socialist Labour Party [SLP] which regarded itself as the party of scientific socialism. It published in pamphlet form many of the writings of Marx, Engels, Kautsky, Prince Kropotkin, Daniel de Leon in America, and others of international fame. These were published at 1d and were complete books. They included the *Communist Manifesto*, *Historical Materialism*, *The Development of Socialism from Utopia to Science*, *Value, Price and Profit*, *Wage-Labour and Capital* and others. These provided working men readers with a background of history and a knowledge of economics which gave many of them an understanding of events superior to that of many of those who controlled events.

An off-shoot of the SLP called itself the British Section of the International Socialist Labour Party – the BSISLP! The members of these bodies did little else than study and discuss these matters and this gave them an intensity of argument that left the more emotional socialists limp. I, of course, argued with them and as often happens, I found many of my ideas romantic and untenable. I had therefore

---

[5]   Rev. John Glasse (1848–1918), writer, minister and socialist, a member of the Social Democratic Federation (SDF) and then the Socialist League, and a correspondent of William Morris. He was appointed to Old Greyfriars in 1877 and resigned his chair in 1909.

to read and study all these aspects to be able to form accurate and sustainable policies. The BSISLP considered themselves the scientists of politics. They did not believe in violence or strikes. Their idea of revolution was to convert everyone to the idea of socialism and when all were agreed, there would be a peaceful revolution where the workers would take over, the capitalists would be absorbed in the new system as managers and other capacities. They allied themselves with the industrial unionism of America whose writer Daniel De Leon was the prophet. Someone once said about socialists that the further left they went the further right they became and certainly, the more revolutionary this group were the more utopian they became.

Amongst the interesting new acquaintances, one stands out – John S. Clarke.[6] John S. Clarke was born in Morpeth with, he said, gypsy antecedents. This appears likely as he had a remarkable power over animals from horses to tigers. He had been a sailor and gone all round the world. He was however a born student and wherever he went he studied life in every form. He had visited the Zulus and was intimate with their history. He was fond of noting the many coincidences in his life. On one occasion he was due to board his ship and, as was customary among seamen, he had spent all his money. When he went on board he was told they would not sail until the next day. He was stranded. He had been in a barber's shop during the day and found that the barber was interested in politics, literature and poetry. Back he went and by selling him his volume of poems, he raised enough to pay for his lodgings overnight. The next time he met the barber was when they both arrived as Labour MPs in Parliament twenty-five years later. He was editing a Christian magazine when he was about fourteen. He had two Royal Society medals for risking his life to save children and when asked if he had anything to show that it was not cowardice that made him refuse to fight, he could refute that in documentary form. He had no fear. When unemployed in Newcastle he got a job as assistant to a lion tamer and discovered a new vocation.

He became a rationalist and came to Edinburgh as a lecturer on rationalism. It was quite a social attraction in salons to have discussions. Bradlaugh,[7] Annie Besant,[8] Professor Huxley[9] and others held great followings and the ideas of Darwin filled the headlines of public controversy. He was a brilliant lecturer and never failed to

---

[6]   John Smith Clarke (1885–1959), politician, journalist and editor, lion-tamer and
      MP for Glasgow Maryhill 1929–31. He was born in Jarrow (not, as AW suggests,
      Morpeth), moved from Newcastle to Edinburgh in 1910 and joined the SLP.
[7]   Charles Bradlaugh (1833–1891), politician and freethinker.
[8]   Annie Besant [*née* Wood] (1847–1933), freethinker, theosophist and politician.
[9]   Thomas Henry Huxley (1825–1895), biologist and science educationist.

fulfil the three basic rules – to attract, to interest and to educate. Then he became a socialist and studied its philosophy and history. We met him first when the Clyde Workers were deported. David Kirkwood, who had been chairman at the famous Lloyd George meeting, Willie Gallacher, Arthur MacManus,[10] and others were arrested in the middle of the night and deported from Glasgow to places of their choice provided they were at least forty miles away from Glasgow. Kirkwood and McManus chose Edinburgh and John S. Clarke and his wife gave them hospitality in their house in Morningside.

We had been arguing about Marx and other subjects with John S. Clarke and were regular visitors at his house and the time of our courtship was largely occupied in this way. He usually opened the discussion with a lecture – he had been lecturing at railwaymen's classes for the Central Labour College – and in addition to socialism, we had lectures on the various aspects of evolution which arose from his rationalism days. We had biological evolution, the evolution of art and script, the evolution of war, the evolution of architecture. He had the most beautiful lantern slides to illustrate all these subjects and I learned the basic lesson of visual aids in teaching. He was also a devotee of music and had a lovely gramophone with a first-class collection of records which gave us all a musical education. In the days before wireless and television, John S. Clarke's house was open house for his friends every Sunday evening when they listened to his records.

A large meeting was held in Pringle's Palace in Leith Walk the night the deportees arrived and it was addressed by John S. Clarke. He could charm an audience just as he could animals, and he aroused passionate indignation at this infringement of human liberty. Kirkwood remained in Edinburgh for some years a prisoner at large of military intelligence. After the war, John S. Clarke went to stay in Glasgow, became the editor of the *Worker*, a Councillor, and the MP for Maryhill. He was a poet and wrote poems after the style of Byron and Burns. As a boy he had won prizes for reciting long poems of Byron. He knew Shakespeare and Burns thoroughly and became one of the greatest authorities on Burns. I used to organise public educational lectures for the Labour College in later years and we could provide an audience of 600 nearly every Sunday to hear his lectures. He had two especially beautifully illustrated lectures on 'Jesus of Nazareth' and 'Robert Burns', when the hall could not hold all those that wanted to attend. With all these gifts one might ask how he did not become a national leader. He was

[10] Arthur MacManus (1889–1927), trade unionist and politician, a member of the SLP and a key figure in the CWC. He played an important role in founding the CPGB and was its first chairman.

not himself an organiser or doer. He was essentially a student and teacher and writer. His book of vitriolic and political poems[11] drew from one reviewer the title of 'The Poet Laureate of Hell'. Ramsay MacDonald gave the poems a great tribute and gained a friend for life. Yet in 1931 John S. wrote an epitaph in my copy:

> Hic Jacet Ramsay Mac
> Friend of all humanity.
> Too many pats upon his back
> Inflated Ramsay's vanity.
> The Blarney stone he often kissed,
> but scattered is his glory:
> for having lived a Socialist
> he died a bloody Tory.

Lives have been written of many people whose adventures and activities were of infinitely less interest than that of John S. Clarke but he created more students out of workers of all kinds in the Labour movement than many more eminent individuals. He, in a way, pioneered the beginnings of the National Council of Labour Colleges (NCLC) which became the largest independent working class educational organisation in the world. At this period, when under the Defence of the Realm Act anyone could be arrested and have his house searched, John S. Clarke parcelled up his valuable collection of revolutionary documents from the time of Cromwell onwards and buried them in a box in waste ground beyond his house in Balcarres Street. I often wonder who dug them up as house building extended years later!

David Kirkwood at that time was a typical good living Calvinistic Glasgow engineer. He was ready to be righteously indignant at any injustice. He stormed into Major Robertson's office at various times to protest at what appeared to him to be bad treatment of COs. He seemed to regard his position of being under the supervision of military authority as authorising him to supervise and keep the military in order. We became lifelong friends and in later years in Parliament I had no more loyal supporter.

My courtship was eventually interrupted by my arrest. It was hardly to be expected that the military authorities would be expert in the law and they frequently blundered into trouble. As a result of improper use by employers of the power to dismiss a worker and make him liable

---

[11] *Satires, Lyrics, and Poems (chiefly humorous)* (Glasgow: The Socialist Labour Press, 1919). Woodburn's inscribed copy is in the collections of the NLS.

to immediate call up, the call up law was amended to allow a period of two months to elapse after a man left his exempted job to permit of his being reemployed by someone else. It was considered wrong to place the power in an employer's hands to decide by dismissing him that he be automatically enlisted. Some COs in Edinburgh had been given absolute exemption on religious and other grounds. The military appealed and the higher tribunal withdrew the exemption. The army then called them up and when they did not appear they were arrested. The COs appealed to the court which decided they had been illegally arrested and they were released. So, when I had left my job to avoid irritation to my firm, it was two months before they could 'call me up'. In due course I was awaited one night by two policemen, taken to the police headquarters and brought before the court in the morning. I was handed over to the military and it was to be three years before I was free.

Barbara and I did meet on several occasions. She was allowed to visit me in the guard room in Glencorse barracks between sentences, I think in the hope that this would persuade me to give up, but when that did not happen they were less generous. It was on one of these visits that we decided to become engaged. I had arranged for Barbara to buy the ring. In prison I was allowed to get a letter and send one once a month. These of course were censored by the governor. Through the help of the chaplain I managed another means of signalling that all was well. Gallacher had been there for some time when I arrived and Kirkwood and others learned that he was working on the roof of the prison and they used to go down to the Calton Hill and they were able to let themselves be seen as a method of encouragement. I found that I could see the steps beside the monumental medallions to Scotland's famous singers and I arranged that at certain times my fiancée would stand there, and by moving the ventilator in my cell window I was able to signal that I had seen her and all was well. Someone must have spotted this for after a time I was shifted to another part of the building. This may all seem rather trivial but when one is shut up in what after all is an elevated dungeon, to have even that small link with civilisation is a brightening experience.

After the war ended a terrible influenza epidemic swept the country and people died in great numbers. My fiancée and her family all narrowly escaped after a severe illness. We, of course, knew nothing about the outside world and chose this moment to go on hunger strike. Dr Devon, the prison commissioner, was worried about this and saw trouble if any of us died. He came to the Calton and asked us to give up and, with the exception of one, we did. He was eventually taken off to the infirmary and had to be forcibly fed. The cause was a protest that although the war had been ended for many months we were being treated with the same rigours as before. In the end there were some relaxations and we were allowed books. In addition to the copy of Marx's *Capital* I have mentioned I obtained books on gold and prices and other economic matters. Reading Marx with care I was struck with the misconceptions which many of his disciples had. I could see the Chaplain's point for, far from Marx condemning 'Capitalism', he analysed it as one of the economic systems by which man had advanced his powers at a greater rate than ever before and which by its very speed of technological change was automatically developing society in the direction of socialism. It made me impatient to get into the midst of controversy and illuminate some of the dark corners in some folk's thinking.

We were released about seven months after the war ended and the little procession that made its way down Waterloo Place towards the post office must have been a queer sight. Barclay the 'Christian' with a beard nearly to his waist and now shuffling along in a dirty old uniform, others in their various garb and myself in civilian garb with a bowler hat and a long Burberry coat, we had decided that our first call was to the post office to send a telegram to Kirkwood, Shinwell,[12] Gallacher and the others who were standing trial as a result of the so-called riot in St George's Square, Glasgow, during a demonstration over 'the forty hours strike'. Kirkwood got off because it was proved that his intervention dissuaded the crowd from throwing an offensive policeman into the river. Gallacher went back into prison for another sentence. Willie Gallacher had been a keen member of the Salvation Army and during the industrial activities of the war troubles on the Clyde he became the Chairman of the Clyde Workers' Committee which became almost an unofficial government in industrial relations. David Kirkwood was a great patriot and all of them would have claimed to be patriots, but in different ways they were nearly all against the war or the way it was being conducted.

The ILP had come out definitely against the war. Snowden[13] and MacDonald both, however, repudiated its attitude. The Social Democratic Federation, the Marxist party, was definitely for the war

[12]   Emanuel Shinwell, Baron Shinwell (1884–1986), politician and trade union-ist, member of the ILP and MP for Linlithgow 1922–4 and 1928–31, Seaham 1935–50, and Easington 1950–70. Shinwell was falsely accused of and imprisoned for instigating the disturbances of 31 January 1919.
[13]   Philip Snowden, Viscount Snowden (1864–1937), politician and MP for Black-burn 1906–18 and Colne Valley 1922–31. Snowden was prominent on the national executive committee of the Labour Party and was Chancellor of the Exchequer in the minority Labour governments of 1924 and 1929–31.

and actually supported conscription as the most democratic way of recruiting an army. They were all definitely against profiteering in the war. Some, of course, held that out of war came revolution. Among these was a John Maclean[14] who in a way was out on his own. He had started the 'Scottish Labour College' in Glasgow where he lectured on Marxian Economics, and he had students from all over Scotland. He had a great following, especially in the Clyde area. The College was ambitiously expected to develop into a residential workers' university. Maclean was one of the many Glasgow socialist teachers who played such a great part in ILP propaganda and he influenced Maxton, I believe, to a considerable extent. When the Russian Revolution took place in 1917 he threw himself wholeheartedly into supporting it.

Prior to the revolution and to the war, Russia had been regarded as a tyranny and everyone was brought up to think of Russia as described in *Resurrection* and *War and Peace*, of political prisoners starting out on the long trek to the torture of life in Siberia. Most people in western Europe were in favour of revolution in Russia and few events in history have been greeted with such a welcome as the overthrow of the Tsar. It is due to this historical atmosphere that there has always been an underlying sympathy for Russia and a tendency to find excuses for all that has happened since. When I went to Spain fifty years after the revolution I explained this to them as the reason why Spain was judged by quite different standards. Franco was the symbol of fascism and all that flowed from that philosophy and this left an atmosphere of antagonism in which it was difficult to get anyone to see any good in dictatorship Spain.

John Maclean was appointed the first Russian Consul in Britain. Unfortunately he became unstable and by the time I saw him in prison he had become the victim of obsessions. As we walked round the ring and I was able to speak with him, he was convinced that the warders were poisoning him and he refused to eat any food. He had already developed this fear at home and it was difficult to get him to eat. John S. Clarke told me that this suspicion had been caused by Petroff,[15] a Russian who had come over to the Clyde before the war to organise

[14] John Maclean (1879–1923), revolutionary socialist and educator, member of the SDF ((later the British Socialist Party (BSP)) and honorary member of the Petrograd Soviet and Soviet consul in Glasgow. Maclean was committed to education of the working classes and founded the Scottish Labour College in 1916. He was imprisoned a number of times during and after the war at both Calton and Peterhead gaols.
[15] Peter Petroff (1884–1947), Russian revolutionary, writer, member of the SDF (later the BSP). Arrived at Leith in 1907 and became a close friend of John Maclean and an important link to Russian revolutionaries and émigré groups. Imprisoned and interned during and after the war.

revolution among the sailors of the Russian battleships being built or repaired there. He said Petroff had convinced him that 'there was a spy behind every lamp post' and that this had become a mania when he became the personification of Russia. I came to know Petroff at a later date when he did a good deal of lecturing in this country. In the interval, he had, of course, been through the Russian Revolution as one of its leaders. He was actually one of the signatories to the Brest Litovsk Treaty. He and his wife had become disillusioned to some extent and came to Britain.

John Maclean never really recovered and after the war, when I became associated with the Scottish Labour College, he thought people had been tampering with examination papers. He was a great personality and probably fell a victim to the strains of the period. There was, of course, a good deal of intrigue and secret service work going on, and a certain amount of agent provocative [*sic*] activity. I recall at a concert in the Usher Hall sitting with friends at a table being joined by some arty-craft types who listened for a while to the talk and then seemed to be diverting the conversation in the direction of securing arms for the Sinn Féin in Ireland. They got short shrift. Even Ramsay MacDonald was nervous about this. We were talking over tea after a conference in Edinburgh and he felt reasonably sure that questions were being put to him at meetings to trap him into saying something which could be built upon. He was not yet back into favour and, of course, he had been persecuted all during the war.

CHAPTER FOUR

The war was over for me and I had to face the future. After all wars there is great political ferment. Feelings about the war were now very mixed. Many had become disillusioned and even embittered. COs experienced curious reactions. They experienced a certain amount of admiration from those who had been convinced by the war itself that they had been cheated by the 'war to end war' slogan, and many, of course, had learned more about its history. On the other hand, most still had the feeling that COs had opted out of taking their share of the battle and a bitter resentment was left.

It would have been easy for me to have thrown myself into politics, as I was advised by some to do, and exploit the sort of halo of heroism which began to attach to those who had gone to prison in resistance to our rulers, but I neither felt a hero nor had any ambitions to fulfil. I had done what I regarded as an unpleasant duty and could not feel that we had really achieved much in the way of stopping wars. I had no desire to become a professional in politics, so I let it rest. I therefore went and had a talk with the head of my old firm, Robert E. Miller. He was really a very fine person. He had been a bit of a socialist himself and had at one time acted as host to Sidney Webb[1] when he came to Scotland in pursuance of his campaign against the old poor law. He did not agree with me in my attitude to the war but had used all his influence to keep me in his firm when the military sought me out. In his flattering descriptions of me when he argued with the military, I think he did much to create the impression that I was a leader of revolt. He himself was willing to take me back but told me that there was still strong resentment among the staff and workers against COs. However, on his advice I went back to my job and on the strength of that security we decided to get married.

---

[1]   Sidney James Webb, Baron Passfield (1859–1947), social reformer and politician, co-founder of the Fabian Society, MP for Seaham 1922–9, held various ministerial appointments in the Labour minority governments.

We had discussed my becoming a teacher and actually I was granted matriculation at Edinburgh University and agreed a course. But this could not fit in with my job. I resumed my interest in the engineering industry. We would have preferred a quiet wedding but our friends determined that it was to be a traditional wedding gathering of the clans. We had expected to stay for some time and enjoy the party but one of my brothers had engineered a send-off and ordered a growler cab to take us away. We had to run the usual gauntlet and scramble into the cab. Whether it is good luck to have mishaps at the beginning or not, we ran into trouble right away. The horse, in its anxiety to get us up the hill at Dundas Street, fell and we had to get out and make our way round the corner into Heriot Row to get out of the way. Someone had pinned a message inside my hat and on brushing off the confetti, my finger was torn on the pin and the blood flowed freely over my hand. We had been unable to get booked anywhere for the honeymoon and spent it quietly at Lower Largo with friends.

During the war there had been pressure on firms to establish efficient costing methods. Many foundry and engineering firms had had only rule of thumb systems. It was now the fashion to have elaborate departments and I was given the job of modernising our methods. This proved a most interesting and practical application of all the theoretical economics I had been studying for some years. After looking into the up-to-date American systems – which, curiously enough, distributed the contribution of buildings, land and machinery almost exactly in the same manner as Marx used to measure the components of value – and the systems used in our own case, I found I had to build a tailor-made arrangement to suit our rather diverse productions. I think I introduced what was probably the first really scientific costing system in this country for foundries producing a large range of castings.

It was, of course, easy to devise a way of costing repetition work according to the published textbooks. I attended on behalf of the firm some lectures arranged by the university on this basis but these were useless for complicated manufacturing. Our own chartered accountants did me the honour of asking permission for their apprentices to see our system at work. Nearly forty years later, a fellow MP asked me to meet one of his constituents, one of these apprentices who had become an accountant somewhere in England, who wanted to visit me and thank me for my help! At first our directors thought my proposals were not as ambitious as was being done in other works. I suggested that one of the first purposes of a costing system should be to cost itself. Costing, in my view, had two main purposes. One was to eliminate the wasteful and unnecessary use of labour or material, and the other was to provide an accurate basis for estimating. Discovering whether completed jobs had been individually profitable was to some extent a luxury form of post mortem unless it contributed to day to day efficiency in supervision. Our system was economical and efficient. The firm were still employing my methods many years after I had left them.

In the political world, the terrible inflation of World War I had made everyone conscious that the manipulation of the currency could nullify past effort and render the savings of a lifetime valueless. I was asked by the ILP to give a lecture on money and it drew a large audience of teachers, business people and many women were there. As a result of this lecture I was asked by a local school of economics to give a series of lectures to a class of miners at Tranent, and this opened a most interesting phase of my political life. I had had, of course, no tutorial help in reading the various books I had studied and I only solved for myself some of the knotty problems by reducing them to terms which I could understand. This, it appears, gave me some success in presenting them in ways which other ordinary people could follow. Whether I had great success in educating the miners or not, one thing is certain – doing the job educated me. The hall I lectured in was both 'lit' and heated by a paraffin lamp and I had difficulty in seeing the students. I had the satisfaction years later of seeing most of these students filling positions as secretaries and officials of their union and for some years most of the local councillors in the district had been members of my classes. I was not allowed to finish at the end of the year. They made me carry on for a good many years and most of my summers were taken up reading and building up lectures for the following session. In the meantime, I was given classes in Edinburgh itself. So, while economics and finance was the basis of my syllabus, I added to their and my own interest other subjects.

I had found that it was almost impossible to explain economics without a good blackboard which used up a good deal of time. When I was asked to give lectures on 'evolution', I had learned from John S. Clarke how valuable lantern slides were. I had none and no money to buy them. The Royal Scottish Museum had a wonderful collection and the director kindly allowed me to look through their collection and borrow those I thought useful. We could not find all I needed but their exhibits of animals etc. were laid out perfectly for my purpose and a young cousin from France who was visiting us and who was a bit of an artist, went with me to the museum and we scratched out on black coated slides pictures and tables to illustrate various points. Later I got a camera and photographed illustrations from books on to slides and many a night I went to bed in the early hours. Sometimes my positives came out negatives or something else went wrong.

I carried over illustration by slides to my lectures on economics and history. It was wasteful to take time in the class to draw charts or balance sheets when this could be done by showing a picture. This had the advantage of getting concentration from the students' eyes, ears and whole attention, for they could see nothing else to divert their eyes. The students appreciated this help and in time they decided to present me with a new lantern to replace the antique one I had bought second hand. When the film strip lantern appeared, that was a godsend. I must have been one of the enthusiastic early users. I could send a set of pictures and get a film strip for about 1d or 2d per slide or frame. I never was able to make my slides an art collection as were those of John S. Clarke. Mine were purely utilitarian and it depended on what I could pick up in second hand collections whether the point was made by the exact picture or one which just fixed it in the memory. A well-known lecturer who visited Edinburgh asked me if he could borrow my slides on 'the industrial revolution'. When he handed them back he said to me he now understood why the Labour College in Edinburgh was such a success – the students had imagination. I believed with Shakespeare that if an object on the stage was described as a chair, the audience's imagination saw a chair. For my purpose, they saw the point.

It is difficult for people now to realise that at that time there was no wireless or television. Education had left most people with a good grasp of the three 'Rs'. The war had, however, shaken everyone out of the rut and all were hungry for knowledge and especially knowledge which would explain that instead of a world fit for heroes to live in which was promised, there was unemployment, attacks on wages and a revaluation of money which brought large firms to ruin, having to wipe 19/- off every £1 of their capital and yet leaving some people millionaires as a result of the war. As many as 120 attended my Sunday morning classes and there were good attendances at the other classes which were run throughout the area and eventually all over the country.

Our tutors and lecturers were in the main amateurs and men and women gave up their time travelling out into the countryside to lecture to miners and others in the various districts. There was no transport as there is today. I had to travel by train to Musselburgh, and then get a little bus to Tranent. Whether I got the train back at Musselburgh at night depended on how long the driver took to say good night to the conductress where he dropped her off half way! One night, Bob Foulis, who stood there for Parliament,[2] and I had to walk back the whole ten miles to Edinburgh.

---

[2]   Robert W. Foulis unsuccessfully contested the Berwick and Haddington constitu-

We were all infused with the purpose of making a new world and we lived to see tremendous changes. It was interesting years afterwards to meet students. I was flattered recently when on two separate occasions on air journeys I met someone who had been a student at these economic classes. Both, curiously enough, had become tycoons handling worldwide commercial affairs running into millions of pounds, and both said all they had accomplished they credited to the fundamental teaching they got in these classes.

I had started my lecturing under the auspices of this local socialist educational group. About this time, John Maclean's illness was making it impossible for him to carry on and J.P.M. Millar,[3] who had also been a CO, became the Secretary of the Scottish Labour College. J.P.M. was one of these people who concentrate everything on one purpose. He had been in the investment department of a big insurance company and because of his training and natural aptitude, had all the characteristics attributed to the Scot of being able to manage money. During an illness as a young man he had been sent to convalesce in the country cottage of a railwayman who was an enthusiast for his union's work in the Central Labour College in London. J.P.M. took one or more courses there and was a student in company with other future leaders of the Labour movement – Jim Griffiths,[4] who became the first Secretary of State for Wales; Aneurin Bevan, who with myself were [sic] destined to have the honour of introducing the National Health Service in England and Scotland respectively; Frank Hodges,[5] who became the leader of the miners; Morgan Phillips,[6] who became Secretary of the Labour Party; Hubert Bowmont [sic],[7] who became Deputy Speaker of the House of Commons; Mark Starr,[8] who became a national figure in the American trade union educational movement, and many others.

ency against John Deans Hope in December 1918.

[3] James Primrose Malcolm Millar (1893–1989), member of the ILP and Edinburgh organiser of the No-conscription Fellowship, imprisoned in Wormwood Scrubs and Wakefield during the war. Millar had been involved in the Scottish Labour College (SLC) since its inception in 1916 and in the early 1920s pressed his vision for weekend and part-time weekday classes against Maclean's for a residential workers' university. Appointed successor to George Sims as secretary of the National Council of Labour Colleges in August 1923.

[4] Jeremiah Griffiths (1890–1975), trade unionist and politician, MP for Llanelli 1936–70, deputy leader of the Labour Party 1956–9, Secretary of State for Wales 1964–6.

[5] Frank Hodges (1887–1947), labour leader and politician, president and secretary of the Miners' Federation of Great Britain 1918–23, MP for Lichfield 1923–4.

[6] Morgan Walter Phillips (1902–1963), labour activist and organiser, National Secretary of the Labour Party 1944-61.

[7] Hubert Beaumont (1883-1948), co-operator and Labour MP for Batley and Morley 1939-48.

[8] Mark Starr (1894-1985), writer and educationalist, author of the popular text *A*

He had been a CO in the interval between his conversion to socialism during his illness and the end of the war when he went to the College. When John Maclean gave up in the Scottish Labour College he took over and he lived and worked for the College until it was the largest independent trade union educational college in the world. The Scottish Labour College and other educational offshoots of the Central Labour College in London were nearly all financed by local effort and fees. J.P.M. Millar applied his insurance principles to the business end of the work and invited trades unions to affiliate to the college on the basis of 2d and later 3d per member per annum, which in theory allowed all the members to attend classes. Of course, only a small number in each union took advantage of the facilities and as usual in such work, many started but few finished the course. This included educational courses by correspondence and/or attendance at classes.

Eventually about 20,000 students were attending lectures and about 20,000 studied by correspondence. Though all the union members who paid did not themselves do the studies, they certainly got the benefit of the education from their fellow workers who did. In ten years, there were throughout industry about 400,000 workers who had studied economics and history, the history of trade unionism, economics, geography, finance, public speaking, trade union law, industrial relations, English and many other subjects, all of which enabled students to acquire methods of thinking in these problems.

Those studies from a working class point of view conflicted with 'orthodox' economics, which tended to explain and justify existing conditions as the best, whereas the workers sought for the building of a world 'nearer to the heart's desire' and Marx's explanation of economic evolution and change gave intellectual justification for their programme of reform. The Workers' Educational Association had done excellent work in extending university education to the general public but it failed to appeal to the great mass of trade unionists by popularising the apologetic economics of Marshall.[9] For example, on one occasion Professor Shield Nicholson[10] wrote to the press during the General Strike of 1926 'proving' that wages should come down without any criticism of a society which denied hope to masses of trade unionists.

It might be wondered how in these circumstances English proved to be one of the most popular subjects taken by correspondence

Worker Looks at History (1917), emigrated to New York in 1928.
[9]   Alfred Marshall (1842–1924), University of Cambridge economist.
[10] Joseph Shield Nicholson (1850–1927), Professor of Political Economy and Mercantile Law at the University of Edinburgh.

course students in the Labour colleges. This arose from the fact that so many workers had left school ill-equipped to express themselves in speech and writing and when they were given responsibility in many of the activities of the Labour movement, they were conscious of their shortcomings. It was difficult for them to go back to classes with people of half their age and the NCLC correspondence courses were designed specially for them. It was soon realised that this course was quite outstanding in the clarity and simplicity of its teaching. Indeed, in the work of the College, the work would have been futile had it failed to be lucid and interesting for there was no obligation on the students to do the work and study.

Young girls who came to work for the English department, often from school, soon obtained from their work as typists etc. such a good knowledge of English that they readily found much better paid jobs in the civil service and other jobs where expert English typists and clerks were required. The College itself suffered from this difficulty. When it had to recruit staff to draft and write the courses, even university graduates on occasion did not measure up to the standard required. The College was under continual fire, being accused of amateurism from its university and WEA opponents, and dared not show failings which could provide ammunition for attack. The credit for the excellence of the correspondence courses, and for the English course in particular, was due in large measure to Christine Hastie – later Christine Millar when she married J.P.M. – who had given up teaching in Edinburgh to join him.

The National Council of Labour Colleges had been formed out of the many local Colleges which had sprung up all over Britain, and J.P.M. Millar had been appointed Press Secretary at its first meeting and then became its General Secretary with headquarters in his home at Elm Row, Edinburgh. From these modest beginnings, by 1963 the NCLC had an affiliated membership of organisations with over thirty million members. It is difficult to exaggerate the influence this encouragement of personal study and thinking by millions of trade unionist members had over the last half century. I should think that every student would in his circle have an informative and steadying influence on at least ten others of his workmates and friends, and this must have insulated millions of people from the tendentious news and views of the capitalist press and also, I found in my own experience helped the workers to make more responsible judgments in industrial relations. It is not impossible that the decline in education about the disasters of inflation in the nineteenth century played some part in the unrealistic and inflationary demands of the seventies!

One indication of the influence this education had had was shown when the first Labour government was formed after the war. It was thought it would be a good idea to hold a dinner of all the new MPs who had been connected with the Labour College before they became MPs. The idea had to be abandoned as there were so many that no place large enough could be found to cater for them. Apart from those who had come up through the university, nearly every MP had been a student, tutor, or official of the NCLC. Many also from the university had been themselves students or were the sons of fathers who had been students. Several Cabinet ministers were generous enough to acknowledge their indebtedness to the help they had had. The work I did in preparing lectures for the class I gave provided me with a wonderful background of knowledge and I can appreciate what they felt. For nearly twenty years before I became an MP, all my spare time and that of my wife were devoted to working in the College and I resisted the temptation to scatter my activities over the many political demands for service which continually cropped up. Even some of my political friends like William Graham, who was, of course, as an MP mostly in London, thought I was a full-time employee of the College.

I was interested mainly in lecturing work, but when the communists thought it would be good business to capture the College, I was roped in to become the Secretary and so became the centre of the organisational work as well. J.P.M. Millar had been at first employed as the full-time lecturer for the College in Edinburgh and he secured his first affiliation in the Mid- and East Lothian Miners. As he had as General Secretary to expand his activities to cover the whole country, Edinburgh and District became more and more my responsibility. Later I became Secretary for the Scottish Labour College which covered all Scotland and with William Elger,[11] Secretary of the Scottish Trades Union Congress, as Treasurer, for many years we 'ran' labour education throughout Scotland. There were occasions when events arose which involved everyone in the Labour movement. On the occasion of the invasion of Russia I served on the 'Hands off Russia' committee.

The ILP in Scotland had affiliated to the Third International which was the logical sequence to the support given by Ernest Bevin, Arthur Henderson,[12] Ramsay MacDonald and others to Russia's overthrow of

---

[11] William Elger (1891–1946), trade unionist and secretary of the Scottish Trades Union Council (STUC) 1922–46.

[12] Arthur Henderson (1863–1935), politician, MP for Barnard Castle 1903–1918, Widnes 1919–22, Newcastle upon Tyne East 1924–31, Clay Cross 1933–5, chief whip 1906–7, 1914, 1920–3, 1925–7, Labour Party Secretary 1912–34, Home Secretary 1924, Foreign Secretary 1929–31.

Tsardom. Illogically, however, at a conference of the ILP in Glasgow, Snowden and others of the National Executive opposed this, and those of us who stuck to our guns became a minority. A conference was held in Sheffield of all the pro-Russian groups and the original Communist Party was formed in Britain. Later, when the Russian Communist Party issued its 'thesis' laying down that every member of the Communist Party was bound to accept without question all decisions of its central executive, there was a general refusal to surrender democratic rights of discussion and the first Communist Party lost its appeal and the modern Communist Party under the Russian thesis came into being. Most of us remained in the ILP which, of course, was not prepared to surrender its rights of decision to Moscow. At a later period, about the time of the Popular Front movement just before the 1939 war, Maxton and the remnant ILP ran for some time in harness with the CP, but Maxton was too wily a politician to obey Communist Party decisions when he would not even accept the decisions of the Labour Party.

In 1924 I had to have an operation and while convalescing I wrote an article for the *Plebs* of which at that time J.F. Horrabin[13] was editor. He was a famous drawer of maps, a strip cartoonist of the *News Chronicle*, and the illustrator of Wells' *Outline of History*. My article dealt with what was, I think, a new idea, of using credit to promote the building of houses. Arising out of this, I was invited to lecture at the *Plebs* summer school on 'finance'. It was held at Cover Hill near Scarborough. Many old friends were there – Ellen Wilkinson;[14] John Jagger,[15] General Secretary of the Distributive Workers; Walton Newbold,[16] and others. After I had explained the credit-system and the working of money I was flattered by the response. Horrabin said he had never previously been able to understand any lecturer on economics but he had actually followed everything I had said and been able to draw his cartoons at the same time. A well-known lecturer of economics at Cambridge told me he had never understood the processes of banking and bookkeeping till I explained the principles behind it. (I could not understand how he had been able to lecture and actually examine – as he did – in economics, if this was so!)

---

[13] James Francis Horrabin (1884–1962), socialist educator and cartoonist. Woodburn was a regular contributor to *Plebs*, the journal of the Plebs League, a workers' education movement that had broken from Ruskin College, Oxford, in 1909.

[14] Ellen Cicely Wilkinson (1891–1947), politician.

[15] John Jagger (1872–1942), trade unionist and politician.

[16] John Turner Walton Newbold (1888–1943), journalist and politician, a driving force in the Plebs League and Labour College movement and the first avowed elected Communist MP when elected for Motherwell in 1922.

Phillips Price,[17] the famous *Manchester Guardian* correspondent during the Russian Revolution, wanted me to tell him where he could get a book which explained it as I had done. I said that so far as I knew, there was none. There was a good deal of pressure that I should do something about it and I promised. Writing a book had never entered my mind but I did write, at their invitation, a pamphlet, *Banks and the Workers*, and I got on with my lecturing.[18]

[17]   Morgan Phillips Price (1885-1973), journalist and politician.
[18]   Arthur Woodburn, *The Banks and the Workers* (London, 1925).

CHAPTER FIVE

The next two years were dominated by the struggle between the miners and the mine owners. Churchill when Chancellor yielded to the pressure to deflate the currency and restore what was called the 'gold standard'. During the First World War, the country changed from basing its transactions on a free circulating currency of gold – sovereigns and half-sovereigns – to one of paper notes. A golden sovereign was about a quarter of an ounce of gold and when the banks issued notes they carried the guarantee that on demand they would replace them by a golden sovereign. This promise was possible only because people did not ask for gold and knew that the bank note was as good as gold. Once war broke out, banks were authorised to provide the money to carry on the war and, of course, there was not enough gold to back up any notes. Money thenceforward was 'paper money'.

After the war the banks wanted to reduce this mountain of paper and restore the balance of paper and gold. I recall attending a meeting where Hartley Withers,[1] one of our leading economists, addressed businessmen appealing to them not to cut down wages which were the basis of a market capable of absorbing the goods they themselves were producing. At the end, the chairman, a prominent businessman, congratulated him on his excellent analysis of the situation. He concluded, however, by saying that 'wages must come down'. The bankers deliberately set out to cut off the money supply that was keeping industry going. The cure was worse than the disease.

The real way to have dealt with the situation was to put the brake on with increasing pressure, but not to jam on the brake and shake the machine to its base. The building of factories stopped in mid-air, great national firms like Baldwins, Armstrong Whitworth and others went bust and had to reconstruct themselves by reducing their capital by about eighty per cent, and generally industry slumped. I remember

---

[1] Hartley Withers, financial journalist, editor of the *Economist* to 1921, then connected principally with the *Saturday Review*.

when controls went off, our foundry had about 1,000 tons of iron in stock for which it had paid £14 a ton. The next day it was worth about £7 a ton and that left a hole in the assets which had to be filled. This deflation spelt ruin to hundreds of firms. Wages had to be reduced to be in keeping with the increased purchasing power of money and resistance to this began the long series of strikes that paralysed much of the productive effort between the wars. Winston Churchill as Chancellor of the Exchequer put our currency back into its pre-war relationship with gold but the price to Britain was catastrophic.

The culmination of these struggles was in 1926 when the miners were practically locked out and the whole trade union movement struck in sympathy in what is known as the 'General Strike'. Although I was not involved personally I was closely in touch with what was happening. Apart from the merits of the strike, the behaviour of everyone concerned was a tremendous tribute to the self-discipline and organising capacity of the ordinary men and women of the land.

All over Britain the strikers formed themselves almost automatically into small units of government, ensuring as far as possible an orderly running of vital services. Not many people had cars in these days but there were volunteers on motor bikes acting as liaison messengers. Committees gave exemptions to hospital and other services of necessity or emergency. There were practically no demonstrations and people kept off the streets. It is difficult to imagine any other industrial country where the situation would not quickly have turned to violence. Although perhaps Winston would have liked some discrediting exhibitions, there were almost none. Of course, many of the men involved had been in the war and some had had experience of exercising responsibility and a large number also had educated themselves by classes and correspondence courses. In the end, however, they answered a question put by the Edinburgh tutor-organiser of the Labour College in a lecture entitled 'can a general strike succeed', which he answered, as did the facts in the negative.

The ILP at this period were seeking some place in the sun of politics and were inclined to be rogue elephants in every situation. At Motherwell, when Chas L. Gibbons[2] was delivering this lecture, an ILP-er questioned what would happen IF everyone came out, IF the police sided with the strikers, and IF the Government could not act, etc. Charlie's reply was that he thought the questioner was in the wrong party – he should join the IFP, the 'if' party.

[2] Charles Gibbons (1888–1967), socialist educator and politician, became Edin-burgh District organiser in 1924, with his remit extended to the East of Scotland in 1928. His lecture on 'The Limitations of a General Strike' was reported in *Plebs*, August 1927.

At our summer school at Scarborough that year, A.J. Cook,[3] the fiery miners' leader, delivered a lecture. Gibbons had been a friend of his in the miners' movement of South Wales and asked him for his notes as a souvenir. To his surprise the notes had nothing to do with the speech A.J. Cook had delivered. Someone said of him that when he rose to speak he had no idea what he would say, when he was speaking he seldom realised what he was saying, and when he had sat down he did not know what he had said. He was really a Welsh evangelist who was carried away by his emotions. While not the wisest of leaders, he could express passionately the miners' feelings.

George Hicks,[4] the General Secretary of the Bricklayers, was an outstanding personality. We were great friends and he had done more than anyone else to put the College on the map of trade unionism. His union had a scheme which cost them about 1/- per member and he transferred the running of it wholesale to the NCLC. The failure of the General Strike knocked the bottom out of resistance to cuts in wages and Ben Turner,[5] textile leader, thought they had to adopt some new approach. He and Sir Alfred Mond,[6] the head of Imperial Chemicals, had discussions and came up with the idea of 'rationalisation' as the new approach to bringing trade unionism and industry up to date. This met with violent controversy. George Hicks became associated with Ben Turner, and then he joined James Maxton and A.J. Cook in the issue of a manifesto with what was called a more left wing approach.[7] They had large meetings all over the country. I had an interesting example of the steadying effect of the educational work we were doing. A bus load of miners from West Lothian who had attended the meeting in the Usher Hall discussed the Maxton-Cook proposals on the road back. They had all attended a lecture I gave on 'the problems of a future Labour government' and they decided, having considered the realities, that the manifesto was impracticable and romantic.

That year George Hicks became chairman of the Trades Union Congress which was holding its conference in Edinburgh. I was asked

---

[3]   Arthur James Cook (1883–1931), trade unionist and ILP member, member of the executive of the Miners' Federation of Great Britain (MFGB) from 1921, and a key figure during the General Strike.
[4]   Ernest George Hicks (1879–1954), trade unionist and politician, a key driver of the amalgamation of the building unions into the Amalgamated Union of Building Trades Workers, of which he was General Secretary 1921–40.
[5]   Ben Turner (1863–1942), trade unionist and President of the TUC 1927–8.
[6]   Sir Alfred Mond (1868–1930), industrialist.
[7]   The 'Cook-Maxton manifesto' was a repudiation of the apparent policy of class collaboration embodied in the Mond-Turner talks and its call for the adoption of a consensual approach to industrial relations. A.J. Cook and J. Maxton, *Our Case for a Socialist Revival* (London, 1928).

to write a history of the trades union movement in Edinburgh and I found the researches most interesting. The Labour movement has always had its troubles over splits and political intrigues, and we know enough from the biographies of Beaverbrook and others what went on in the other parties, but nothing could compare with the manoeuvres and intrigues I discovered in the politics of the Church in the struggle for power. The General Assembly was probably the most powerful democratically elected body in the world, but power to a large extent still rested in the hands of the bishops representing the king. The reformers had to circumvent the power of their veto. One of the rules was that no one accused of any crime could attend the Assembly. So the reformers promptly accused every bishop of all the crimes they could think of, and especially the type of crime that would also smear their reputation. The bishops were in this way excluded from the Assembly and the changes were carried without opposition. Character assassination is not a modern invention.

Robert E. Miller, the chairman of our firm, took a philosophic interest in social and political problems. In his younger days he had been host to Sidney Webb when he visited Scotland in the campaign on poor law reform. He was therefore very tolerant of my activities in the Labour College and Labour Party. He asked me if I could get him a ticket for one of the interesting debates in the TUC. I asked J.R. Clynes[8] for his advice and he warned me off a day when there was going to be trouble, but this was the day 'Bertie', as we called the boss, decided to go. He gave me his impressions which were a remarkable assessment of the personalities of the time. He thought A.J. Cook was inconsequential, Clynes was a statesman, J.H. Thomas[9] limited in his vision, 'Citrine'[10] had delivered a speech which would have graced any assembly in the world, and Hicks had made an admirable and masterly chairman. He enjoyed the fight.

The pioneers of the modern socialist movement were still active when I became involved and it was both an experience and an honour to have known them. Most of them had been born in poverty and like Keir Hardie,[11] had been fired with righteous indignation at the conditions under which people were forced to live. It is hardly possible

---

[8] John Robert Clynes (1869–1949), trade unionist and politician, MP for Manchester North East 1906–18 and Manchester Platting 1918–1931, 1935–45, Home Secretary in the Labour government 1929–31.

[9] James Henry Thomas (1874–1949), trade unionist and politician, MP for Derby 1910–36.

[10] Walter McLennan Citrine, first Baron Citrine (1887–1983), trade unionist and public servant, General Secretary of the TUC 1925–46.

[11] James Keir Hardie (1856–1915), founder of the Labour party, MP for West Ham South 1892–5, Merthyr Tydfil 1900–15.

for people now to imagine what went on in Britain unless they visit the slums of undeveloped countries. Great improvements had been made by the efforts of these men, but until the last war, it was still possible to describe our country as 'a land where wealth accumulates and men decay'. A historian of the period before 1914 in her description of working-class conditions picks on one example among others where children could not all go out at one time because they had to take turnabout of the available clothes. Actually, my wife as a teacher in Leith had a case in her class when two children came on alternative days because only one set of garments was available. Teachers also had the job of gathering clothes and the Tory government of the day issued a regulation that children were to be supplied with boots only after they had been certified as suffering from malnutrition.

One can see how much worse things were before unemployment benefit and national insurance were introduced in 1912. Desperation made [it] unsafe for people to be on lonely roads or in the dark, even in a well-to-do town like Edinburgh. In Glasgow we heard about cases where in one room when a baby died, its little coffin was shifted backwards and forwards from the bed to the table. There was no other room. Dockers fought each other at the gates for jobs. Between the wars, we had the conditions described in *Love on the Dole*[12] and a whole generation of children grew up without being able to find a job, demoralised by misery and idleness, and denied even the benefits of unemployment benefit by what appeared, in theory, as reasonable: that they could not prove they had been genuinely seeking work which did not exist. Men like Keir Hardie, J.R. Clynes, Will Thorne[13] and others rose to be leaders in trades unions and politics, and Clynes and Keir Hardie became leaders of the Labour Party.

Will Thorne and Clynes were still MPs when I went to Parliament and it was a curious feeling to be there hearing quite a number of these old leaders speaking when a few years previously, I had been lecturing about their achievements in the history of the trades union movement. I was therefore able to appreciate the feeling of new members who arrived during my time, many of whom had read my articles and books on socialism and economics or been students in the Labour College and found me still alive and kicking. Clynes had to teach himself English by reading William Cobbett's book[14] in a candlelit

12 Walter Greenwood, *Love on the Dole: A Tale of Two Cities* (London, 1933), an influential novel in shaping responses to and memories of the interwar period, which was later made into a play and a film.
13 William James Thorne (1857–1946), trade unionist and politician, MP for West Ham South 1906–18 and Plaistow 1918–45.
14 William Cobbett, *Grammar of the English Language* (1818).

garret. Will Thorne and others learned in their fights to establish a living wage. Tom Mann[15] and others from the craft unions were a kind of aristocracy. Their energy and leadership changed the face of Britain. Clynes, the reformer, Tom Mann, the revolutionary, and Ben Tillett:[16] these three shared with Lloyd George the power of a silver voice and a capacity for clear and deadly logical argument. As was said about Citrine, their speeches would have graced any assembly in the world. Another of these outstanding personalities was George Lansbury. He was a great missionary and in his speeches he, as it were, embraced everyone in a great Christian hug. We were all truly brothers to him and he was reluctant to face the realities of human wickedness in the threats of Hitler.

Perhaps this was summed up in 1936 when the Labour Party at its conference in Edinburgh was deciding that it must recede from its role of disarming and face up to the dictators. Standing in the gangway while Stafford Cripps[17] was putting the argument about the Spanish Civil War in Spain, he said 'Arthur, maybe this must be done, but I am not the man to do it'. When he went on deputations to ministers they used to split the delegation by saying 'We know, of course, Mr Lansbury, that this is not your personal view'. This became too much for Ernest Bevin[18] and Hugh Dalton,[19] who knew about Hitler's preparations for war, and Bevin made a speech at the party conference which forced his resignation. He had been on the poor law commission with King Edward and it could truly be said of him that he could walk with kings and keep the common touch.

---

[15] Thomas Mann (1856–1941) trade unionist, socialist and communist, member of the SDF, joined the CPGB on its formation and in 1921 became first chairman of the British section of the Red International of Labour Unions.

[16] Benjamin Tillett (1860–1943), trade unionist and politician, prominent role in great dock strike of 1889 and in foundation of the Labour Representation Committee, MP for Salford North 1917–24, 1929–31.

[17] Sir Richard Stafford Cripps (1889–1952), politician and lawyer, joined Labour party in 1929, MP for Bristol East 1931–50, Bristol South East 1950. Chairman of the Socialist League from 1933, he was expelled from the Labour Party in 1939, but rejoined in 1945. Solicitor-general 1930–1, British Ambassador to the Soviet Union 1940–2, President of the Board of Trade 1945–7, Chancellor of the Exchequer 1947–50.

[18] Ernest Bevin (1881–1951), trade unionist and politician, MP for Wandsworth Central 1940–50, Woolwich East 1950–1, Minister of Labour and National Service 1940–5, Foreign Secretary 1945–51, Lord Privy Seal 1951.

[19] Edward Hugh Neale Dalton, Baron Dalton (1887–1962), economist and politician, MP for Camberwell Peckham 1924–31, Bishop Auckland 1935–59, President of the Board of Trade 1942–4, Chancellor of the Exchequer 1945–7, Chancellor of the Duchy of Lancaster 1948–59, Minister of Housing and Local Government 1950–1.

The early orators of the Labour movement learned their public speaking the hard way. There were no captive audiences. They had to be attracted and often they were hostile and even violent when they were asked to do something to improve their conditions. There was a large and there still remains today a deferential section [*sic*] of the population whose attitude to the rich and the aristocracy has changed little from feudal days. Poverty and misery held such terrors for people that anyone who gave a man a job was a benefactor and it was thought that any suggestion of revolt was likely to end in a terrible retribution. As we know from today's suspicions of the workers about any suggestion to change industrial relations, the people have long memories.

The most successful street speakers were those that could attract and then interest the crowd. After that they could instruct and educate them. Bernard Shaw learned to do his speaking on the street and no doubt he also learned there the power of his 'blarney' as a vehicle for his propaganda. In less turbulent days I did my share of street speaking although I did not like it and it became impracticable with the coming of motor buses and traffic congestion. One of the most famous of this type of speaker was Jack Jones[20] who later became the MP for Silvertone. He used to have a striking phrase to attract a crowd such as 'I come from poor but honest parents; if they had not been so honest they would not have been so bloody poor'. Sometimes it was 'poor but bibulous parents'.

Tom Wilson,[21] who became a Glasgow councillor, was another example of ingenuity. He was organiser for the shop assistants. A union had been formed and Will Y. Darling, who later became the Lord Provost of Edinburgh and one of its MPs, was the runner up for the post of its General Secretary. Shop assistants were difficult to organise. To join a union was usually to leave a job! Tom Wilson, however, promoted a strike in one of the large fashionable stores in Glasgow. The parade of strikers with their banners did not seem to have much effect. Tom Wilson went to Jim Larkin,[22] the famous Irish dock leader, and got him to get about a thousand of his dockers to line up at the shop to buy something such as 1d of elastic. This, of course, caused chaos and no ordinary customers could get near the shop. Soon 'reason' prevailed and the strike was settled.

---

[20] John Joseph Jones (1873–1941), trade unionist and politician, MP for West Ham
       Silvertown 1918–40.
[21] President of the STUC 1924.
[22] James Larkin (1874–1947), labour leader in Ireland, ILP member, founder of Irish
       Transport and General Workers' Union 1908.

Will Y. Darling was himself a character, an original in many ways. He was a nephew of one of the owners of one of the largest drapery stores in Edinburgh's Princes Street. He had gone to London and got a job at Whiteley's, the big emporium. In these days apprentices, and seemingly floor walkers like Will, slept on the premises. Will Y. became active as a shop assistant trade unionist and became an eloquent speaker at open air meetings on the street. It was called to Whiteley's attention that Will was a political agitator and he was called before the boss for an explanation. Will explained to Mr Whiteley that their contract was that he sold his labour for ten hours a day to Whiteley's. For the rest of the time Will felt free to do and speak as he liked. Mr Whitely disagreed and Will found himself out of a job. So in his tile hat and frock coat, he paraded in front of the store as a victimised shop assistant with sandwich boards proclaiming the fact. He then started to tramp his way back to Scotland.

On the way, he was said to have been arrested as a vagrant having no visible means of subsistence. He delivered a great oration to the magistrate and pointed to the fact that he had bought a barrel organ with which to earn his keep. He later wrote a book *Down and Out* [sic][23] where he illustrated how an intelligent person could have a very cultured life in this capacity – getting breakfast at some charity, studying in the public library, scraping a lunch, and having tea etc. for 6d in one of the stores, which also provided the evening paper. He got a job selling fire extinguishers. He persuaded an insurance company that if they made him their manager in Dundee he could treble their business – and he did. However, he went off to the First World War, was there with Churchill, came back to be intelligence officer to Sir John Anderson[24] at the time of the Black and Tans in Dublin, came back to Edinburgh to become its Lord Provost and one of its MPs. He in Edinburgh and Sir Patrick Dollan[25] in Glasgow both probably created records in the amount of press space they occupied during their terms of office. They were among the picturesque personalities of their generation.

The failure of the General Strike and the forcing of the miners back to work after about six months' starvation turned the eyes of everyone to the next election when the government could be held responsible.

[23] William Y. Darling, *Down but not out: being the true story of Peter Gogg* (London, 1935).
[24] Sir John Anderson, first Viscount Waverley (1882–1958), civil service administrator and politician, MP for Scottish Universities 1938–50, Lord Privy Seal 1938–9, Home Secretary 1939–40, Lord President of the Council 1940–3, Chancellor of the Exchequer 1943–5.
[25] Sir Patrick Joseph Dollan (1885–1963), journalist and politician, ILP member and prominent figure in Glasgow politics, sitting on the town council 1913–46 and serving as Lord Provost 1938–41.

The first Labour government in 1924 had made clear to everyone that some problems were international. Sovereignty was limited in all sorts of ways. Reparations – 'make Germany pay' – had proved a disaster and the first crack was in Germany's inability to pay interest on the huge loans she had had from America. This dislocated the finances of the international world and had much to do with the crash in the United States which reverberated through Britain and the other world exchanges.

About 1928 I gave a course of lectures on 'finance' – with a history and explanation of the role of money, how industry, local authorities and the nation raised their funds, the role and limits of credit, etc. I felt it was incomplete without giving some idea of socialist finance. In my innocence, I thought I had nothing to do but to study what had been written on this subject. I had put the title into the syllabus for the last of the twelve lectures but discovered to my dismay that there was practically nothing available for consultation. Most socialist writers had been more concerned about getting the power to introduce socialism than to think about what would be the practical problems which would arise. I found that I had to think the transition out for myself. A lecture which I thought I could prepare in about a fortnight took me nearer six months.

That series of lectures was delivered to a packed class of about one hundred students every Sunday morning and, of course, everything I said was subject to cross-examination and discussion. As a result, my ideas were severely tested. The students came from Edinburgh and the surrounding centres of population and I found myself busy giving a lecture all over the place on 'problems of a Labour government'. Prior to that most people had rather a utopian view of Labour in power. I was interested to find that, though I felt I was discouraging them with the difficulties we would have to face, on nearly every occasion the audience at the end raised additional problems they had seen. I recall Manny Shinwell who took the chair at one of these lectures confessing to the shock of being faced with realities. It was listening to this lecture and discussing it that made the miners at the Cook-Maxton Manifesto meeting decide that their programme was romantic nonsense and totally impracticable.

I was pressed to write a textbook on the basis of these lectures and this was published as *The Outline of Finance*.[26] This book went all through the Labour movement and, as it happened, it became a godsend when the 1931 general election was fought on the 'gold

---

[26] Arthur Woodburn, *Outline of Finance* (London, 1930). Published as no. 6 in the 'Plebs textbooks' series, it went through a number of subsequent editions.

standard'. One MP said he cursed me several times during the election for having had such a poor index for he had to read the book time and time again to find the answer to some question which he knew was there. Hugh Dalton, Labour's first Chancellor of the Exchequer after the war, wrote in a preface: 'This little book is a masterpiece of condensation. Hardly anything of importance within the field is left out and there are many references for further reading. The so-called mysteries of high finance are summarily laid bare.'

That was certainly the purpose of the book. In any case, very few people at the time had given any real thought to the subject. As I said to the Macmillan Committee,[27] if the ramifications and influence of finance on industry and society were understood, there would be no need to set up a commission to explain them. Indeed, it was said by a well-known economist that there were about four people who really understood the workings of finance. Certainly, the number whose books helped me to a clearer grasp was very few. So by one of these chances in history, the book was in circulation when the great financial crisis hit the world and the Labour candidates in the 1931 election in the main had some background on which to discuss the question intelligently.

But that was like whistling in a thunderstorm. An ex-Tory Minister started the great 'savings bank scare' and the Coalition government under Ramsay MacDonald was swept back to power to 'save the pound'. (Incidentally the pound was devalued soon afterwards.) I had fought South Edinburgh for Labour in 1929. This was the first occasion that South Edinburgh had had a Labour candidate. It was considered one of the safest Tory seats in Scotland. We had crowded meetings and as the audiences were mostly professional and executive types I was subjected to questions which called for reasoned and informed answers. [I saved my deposit by only fifty votes. This, a member of the Conservative Club wrote to tell me, was a triumph. Lest I preened myself too much about that, I got a corrective in 1935 when my wife beat my vote in the same constituency!]

---

[27] Treasury committee on finance and industry 1929–31, chaired by Hugh Pattison Macmillan, Baron Macmillan (1873–1952).

CHAPTER SIX

The financial crisis struck this country between 1929 and 1931 when Labour was in power. Winston Churchill later called it an economic blizzard. What had happened was that after the First World War there was a stupid slogan of 'make Germany pay'. Germany had paid by borrowing from us and the United States. In 1923 inflation in Germany had reached such an extremity that people were paying for their entry into cinemas with pieces of coal – money was valueless and unacceptable. At one time thirty-three printing works and twelve paper mills were occupied with the making and printing of notes. When the mark was stabilised, one dollar could buy 4,500,000,000,000 marks! Germany could not meet the interest on the huge loans she had had and this started off an avalanche of failures.

In our own country, there was a speculative boom in which a company promoter named Clarence Hatry[1] was the outstanding figure and his crash was a further factor in the upset of confidence in money as a reliable measure of value. The German banks started to fail: there was a crash in the United States in which millions of people were ruined; and the whole question of the value of the pound also became involved.

In 1928 a Labour newspaper was established in Edinburgh – the *Labour Standard*[2] – and till it ended some three years later, I wrote every week a signed article on political events. Its editor James Dunbar, who was a civil servant, turned ill just before the Leith by-election and I had to take over. I was met with a demand from the printer for payment of his account so my first job was to get its finances reorganised. During the Leith by-election, I wanted to print telling cartoons. I drew the first one myself and at a meeting the following week I was approached by a draughtsman-artist offering to do cartoons. I said I had arranged for

---

[1] Clarence Charles Hatry (1888–1965), company promoter, sentenced to fourteen years' penal servitude in 1930 and released in 1939.
[2] The *Labour Standard* was published 1925–30.

one every week until the election by an artist in Glasgow. He said he was very glad for the one the previous week – which was mine – had been terrible!

When, in 1929, I was approached to stand for South Edinburgh, I said I did not want to become involved in the political side as one could not do everything. However, I was pressed on the grounds that I had no right teaching others what to do and not doing it myself. So I agreed and began the campaign. We had no money and ran a sale of work which James Maxton came through to open, and with the £120 we raised we managed to pay the election deposit of £150. Before that we had raised odd sums by jumble sales. I had to go round in my car on one occasion, for example, collecting old junk for the sale from which we raised about £5. My election agent had to go to his normal work all the time of the election so I had really to be candidate, public relations officer and agent at the same time. The election was fought in May during the time of the General Assembly and I can recall rushing back to work from a mid-day meeting passing the then duke of York – the Lord High Commissioner – and the duchess – now the Queen mother – in the King's Park as they drove in the other direction.

I was at work daily during the time of the election. It rather tickled the head of our firm that I was a Labour candidate. He suggested I should not be too hard on the capitalists. One of the issues at the election was the League of Nations and it was extremely damaging to the Conservatives that Lord Robert Cecil,[3] one of the Tory Ministers, had resigned as their representative at the League of Nations because of what he regarded as his own government's insincerity in their attitude to the League.

I became more and more involved in politics and in 1928, I had attended my first Labour Party conference. We had lost the Leith by-election in March. The National Executive had insisted that Bob Wilson,[4] the candidate, sign an undertaking to stick to Labour Party policy. At a meeting which I chaired in Fisherman's Hall, Newhaven, he had answered a hypothetical question thrown suddenly at him, indicating that he would be in favour of confiscation. There was such a furore about it and, as there was little over one hundred votes between him and victory, it was generally assumed that his blunder had lost us the election. The National Executive were also annoyed that the Leith

---

3   Robert Gascoyne-Cecil, Viscount Cecil of Chelwood (1864–1958), President of the League of Nations Union 1923–45, resigned as Chancellor of the Duchy of Lancaster in August 1927 and asked the electorate in 1929 to vote for pro-League candidates.
4   Robert Freeman Wilson, socialist and Leith newsagent.

Labour Party had not accepted Wedgwood Benn[5] who had come over to Labour, when, because he thought it was the right thing to do, he resigned to fight the seat again under his new colours.

At the next conference in Birmingham I had discussions with George Shepherd,[6] Arthur Henderson and George Lansbury about this demand for a signature, and I persuaded them to agree that if Bob Wilson told me he was adhering to the programme, that would be sufficient. When the matter came before the Leith party someone misrepresented what had occurred and said I had been asked by the Executive to get Bob Wilson 'to give in', so the arrangement fell through. No wonder Bernard Shaw said that we should have had socialism long ago but for the socialists. Ernest Brown had held the seat easily in 1929. I was approached by a Leither to stand as a person perhaps likely to get all sections behind me, but the election fell in the middle of the 1931 crisis and although up till the crisis started there was considerable hope of pulling it off, Ernest Brown,[7] however, was saved by the scare that Labour would take the people's savings. This gave the Tories victory all over the country.

Shortly after this I had a visit from Ben Shaw[8] who was the Scottish Secretary of the Labour Party. He was due for retiral and was anxious about his successor. He said he could think of only two people who would fill the bill – A.B. Mackay,[9] a banker in Glasgow, and myself. A.B. had a son going through the university and he said it would not be easy for him to make the sacrifice so he had boiled it down to me. I pointed out I was already quite happy with my own job and the work I could do voluntarily and that I was not keen to become too much involved. I knew what the movement was. It got you in by the sleeve, then the arm, then the body and soul as well. I wanted to belong a little to myself. I then had a phone message from William Elger, Secretary of the Scottish Trades Union Congress, to the same purpose. I finally agreed to write George Shepherd, the National Agent, telling him that

[5] William Wedgwood Benn, first Viscount Stansgate (1877–1960), politician, MP for Tower Hamlets 1906–18, Leith 1918–28, Aberdeen North 1928–31, Manchester Gorton 1937–42, Secretary of State for India 1929–31, Secretary of State for Air 1945–6.
[6] George Robert Shepherd, Baron Shepherd (1881–1954), political organiser, national agent of the Labour Party 1928–46.
[7] Ernest Brown (1881–1962), MP for Rugby 1923–4, Leith 1927–45, Secretary of State for Mines 1932–5, Minister of National Service 1935–40, Secretary of State for Scotland 1940–1, Minister of Health 1941, Chancellor of the Duchy of Lancaster 1943, Minister of Aircraft Production 1945.
[8] Benjamin Howard Shaw (1865–1942), politician, ILP member and first Secretary of the Scottish Advisory Council of the Labour Party 1914–32.
[9] Key figure in the formation of the Scottish Bankers' Association in 1919.

if they could not find anyone else and they regarded it as necessary for me to take on the job, I'd do so.

This was in 1932. My wife and I decided to take a trip to Russia with Intourist to see what was happening there. We left from Hay's Wharf London in the *Cooperatzia* and sailed to Leningrad. For a solid thirty-six hours, all but a few on board were sea-sick and it made us worse to see people like my brother-in-law eating their meals as if they were on shore. However, when we passed into the Kiel canal, everything became enjoyable and the boat then became a huge debating society. There were professors from universities in America, Africa and elsewhere. There were Russian exiles returning to see the new country and a great many university dons from this and other countries. Hitler had not yet seized power in Germany but as we passed along the canal, a young student from Oxford – his father was a general in the British army – was shouting to the Germans on shore 'rote front'.

There were a good many enthusiastic communists on board. Nearly all, however, were sympathetic to this great experiment we were going to see. I had a stiff job defending the Labour Party line in Britain and was under severe bombardment from people from many countries. I recall talking to a professor of mathematics from somewhere in the States and I happened to mention that I did not know a great deal about mathematics except so far as I had needed calculations for engineering purposes. He said I may not know it, but in one way I was an excellent mathematician for he had been listening to my arguments and was of the opinion that I was the best logician on board. I was very flattered but I am afraid I had to confess that I had not realised that logic was mathematics!

Before we finished the trip, I had often to explain to the idolators of Russia how it was unreasonable to expect that a country so lately emancipated from poverty and backwardness could be completely changed in such a short time. One communist was horrified to be charged commission when he bought a postage stamp and others were shocked to see people drunk. A revolution does not necessarily make everyone teetotal. We travelled from Leningrad to Moscow, then to the Volga to Nizhny-Novgorod, later to be called Gorki, where Ford's were cooperating in erecting modern car factories, and then sailed down the Volga to Kineshma, a cotton town, and back to Leningrad.

While I was away, the Labour Party had been holding a selection for their new Scottish Secretary and on my return, I found the post-card inviting me to attend. As the date was passed, I assumed the matter had all been settled and that someone had been found. I heard no more until in the beginning of September I received a telegram asking me to meet the Executive of the Labour Party at Newcastle where the Trades Union Congress was meeting. I found there was another possible appointee present and I explained to the National Executive that I really was not seeking the position and would rather they found someone else. Only if they were in serious difficulty and could not find anyone suitable was I prepared to agree. Their answer was unanimously to appoint me.

Had it not been that my wife and I had no family and that our whole interest apart from my regular occupation was now concentrated in the Labour movement, I should not have agreed, but I realised that a difficult position existed in Scotland and that I did have some advantages in tackling it. I was known all over as the Secretary of the Scottish Labour College. I knew the ILP, the CP and all the other Ps which were preventing a united Labour Party. It meant my giving up the candidature at Leith, where we had just healed the breaches made over the Wilson affair, but I stipulated that I should continue with the educational work as far as practicable for I was convinced that, though less spectacular, it was more permanent than day to day propaganda. This was agreed to and so we had the interesting position that I was Secretary of the Labour Party and Secretary of the Scottish Labour College. William Elger was Secretary of the Scottish Trades Union Congress and Treasurer of the Scottish Labour College, so between us we had the possibility of keeping the movement in Scotland going harmoniously.

But there were formidable difficulties. There was practically no Labour Party in Scotland. The Labour Party was still largely a federated body and the real drive was in the ILP. But the ILP had just broken away from the Labour Party and my job was practically to build from scratch.

Pat Dollan, Tom Johnston and others, however, had formed the Scottish Socialist Party (SSP) to try and carry over to a loyal body those ILP-ers who had not disaffiliated. Tom Johnston did not remain in it long and came soon into the Labour Party. Arthur Brady became Secretary and a good many prominent members of the ILP such as Andrew Gilzean[10] and James Hoy[11] in Edinburgh were on the Executive. Meantime, the disaffiliated ILP continued to function. When it was known that the ILP were breaking away, I was approached by James Hoy and others of the Edinburgh Central ILP for advice as to how they could retain their funds for the Labour Party.

[10] Andrew Gilzean (1877–1957), politician and ILP member to 1932, then Vice-chairman of SSP, MP for Edinburgh Central 1945–51.
[11] James Hoy (1909–76), politician, MP for Leith 1945–50, Edinburgh Leith 1950–70, Parliamentary Private Secretary (PPS) to the Scottish Office 1947–50.

By a freak of chance, I was one of the few people who knew what would happen under the law, for in my early experience in connection with the litigation over the 'Wee Frees', I was able to tell them that unless they alienated the property and funds before the disaffiliation, any continuing members of the branch who remained in the ILP would be able to claim all the funds. I advised them to form a trust in the Central Labour Party and transfer the hall and funds right away. They went away to do this but Brady came through from Glasgow and assured them the position would be all right and they did not proceed, with the result that about three or four members of the Central ILP, who had not been long in the branch, laid claim to and obtained the property. The SSP took the case to the courts and the decision was made on the precedent of the church case in 1904 with which I had been connected. So halls and property all over Scotland which had been accumulated by the sacrifice and work of hundreds of people were all lost, for many of those who got them never used them for their original purpose and they were frittered away in various ways.

But the existence of the SSP was an additional complication in the work I had undertaken. They were all good friends of mine and loyal to the Labour Party, but the existence of the SSP meant that Labour Party workers were divided and that the work was duplicated in many towns and villages. Pat Dollan, who was the driving force of the SSP, was also the Scottish editor of the *Daily Herald*. Publicity was vital to the building up of the Labour Party as well as the SSP, but the SSP had the advantage of me, with Pat in command of the channel of news. He did not stop mine getting in but the harder I worked and the more success I had was a stimulation to him to keep up the end of the SSP. When I called a conference, it required more than a month to give the trades union branches time to meet and send delegates, but Pat could jump the gun and call the conference on the same subject within a fortnight, give the SSP the earlier publicity and leave mine to trail along behind.

On the other hand, I had real battles on with the ILP and the Communist Party. I was convinced that if I supplied the weapons our people would fight, so a good deal of my effort was put into articles in the *Forward*, providing the reasons why the movement could succeed only if it were united. I lectured all over, and attended business meetings – I have had to attend and speak at three meetings on a Sunday miles apart. I knew that if I got the seeds of the Labour Party planted they would grow and I put years of work into these early months for this purpose. In the end, SSP members appreciated the wasted effort of duplicating meetings, and branches one after another dissolved and became Labour parties. I never told them to do so but I said it did seem a waste of energy doing the same job twice – once as the SSP and then as the Labour Party to make it official. There was one amusing example of this process.

In the House of Commons before the split, out of 288 MPs on the Labour side, 142 were claimed as ILP members. The Easter conference of the ILP that year had instructed its National Administrative Council to reconstruct this ILP group of members on the basis of acceptance of ILP policy as distinct from Labour Party policy. The ILP then issued a demand to ILP MPs to accept this decision of the Easter conference as a condition of their continuing to be members of the ILP in Parliament. This placed MPs in the dilemma of having two groups deciding policy and tactics with the possibility that they could come to contradictory decisions. The result of this demand was that only fourteen out of the 142 ILP members adhered to the ILP group led by James Maxton. At the 1931 Conference of the Labour Party, the ILP proposals were defeated by 2,117,000 to 193,000.

The fact of the matter was that the Labour Party had grown up and no longer had its policy decided for it by the ILP within it. This robbed the ILP of its privileged position of leadership. If the ILP was to retain a separate existence, it had to find a role to play. It might have taken over the propaganda work for which it had proved a great instrument, but James Maxton and his friends preferred to establish what was, in effect, a rival party with separate leadership and a different policy. Very often, looking back, it seemed that the only purpose of counterproposals to those of the Labour Party was to be different.

I personally had lost confidence in James Maxton whom I had admired very much. It was at the first national conference I attended. This was at Birmingham in 1928. One incident I recall. Maxton had accused MacDonald of having been more concerned about giving pensions to the staff of the Foreign Office than to the old age pensioners. MacDonald replied from the platform saying that when Maxton made that statement, he knew he was stating what was untrue because Maxton was at the meeting where MacDonald had explained that the Foreign Office were treated differently from all other civil servants and were privileged. What he had done was to bring them into line with the rest of the civil service.

Another incident had disillusioned me about Maxton's so called 'left wing' attitude. Willie Graham, Maxton and others had been appointed to a committee by the ILP to examine the possible effects of compensation and confiscation in the pursuit of nationalisation. The committee went carefully into the matter and, with the exception of Maxton, had signed a report in favour of compensation as the best practical policy. Maxton had signed a minority report in favour of confiscation. But Willie Graham told me that Maxton had not even attended the meetings of the committee.

Maxton, however, was a great evangelical orator and could hold an audience with his personal magnetism. In Parliament also, he was by far the finest dramatic actor on that stage and Winston Churchill sometimes looked on him with admiring envy. He was a great favourite personally but preferred the role of prophet to that of practical statesman. He had a mischievous sense of humour and used to delight in throwing a cat among the pigeons. I have seen him egging David Kirkwood to extravagances. He made the balls and David Kirkwood fired them. The final result was that the ILP established itself as a small but separate policy-forming group in Parliament.

It caused a split in the constituencies and lost us a good many people who gave up all participation in politics in disgust or despair. In Maryhill, a meeting of the ILP was held to demand an explanation from its MP, John S. Clarke, as to why he had not complied with the ILP demand. He said, 'after hearing the speeches tonight all I have to say is that you had better get another Member of Parliament for I am fed up with the bloody place anyhow'. The net eventual result was that Maryhill almost to a man turned over to the Labour Party and became one of the strongest branches in Scotland. This recalls another episode in JSC's candidature. He was holding a large open air meeting and was being heckled by communists in the audience. Asked one of their stock questions at the time 'why had Margaret Bondfield[12] signed the Blanesburgh report?', he said 'We might as well have all the stock questions – "why did the Labour Government send troops to China?", "why did Ramsay McDonald bomb Iraq?" My answer to them all is quite simple "I don't know!"'

It was in this atmosphere that I took on the job of persuading people to build up the Labour Party in Scotland. It meant persuading them to give up other parties. I have always said we cannot bully people into socialism and many of the individuals in the communists, ILP and SSP were first-class workers. All that was wrong was their sense of direction. One of my great instruments was the columns of the *Forward*, where week by week I carried on polemic discussions on the theories that were dividing us. Everyone started out by wanting unity and finished by making disunity. My thesis was that unity demanded one policy, one leadership and one party, and that could be achieved

[12] Margaret Grace Bondfield (1873–1953), trade unionist and politician, MP for Northampton 1923–4, Wallsend 1926–31, Minister of Labour 1929–31. Her support for funding unemployment benefits from contributory insurance rather than from general taxation and the restriction of benefits (measures embodied in the Blanesburgh report of 1927) was controversial within the Labour movement.

only by democratic discussion and, if necessary, by majority vote. For the purpose of argument, I accepted the assumption that those who were, as they believed, 'on the left' of the Labour Party were more brilliant and more 'advanced' than the trade union masses of the Labour Party, but then what was the purpose of these leading minds cutting themselves off from the mass that needed them and rushing ahead of the main army? I showed the communists from their own accepted philosophy that they were acting wrongly.

Quotations from Lenin were deadly ammunition. When he was replying to those who objected to paying compensation and giving big salaries to specialists, he said 'it would be an obvious mistake to give free rein to shouters and phrasemongers who allow themselves to be attracted by dazzling revolutionism'. The very title of his attack 'the childishness of the left' was an important slogan against slogans. Both Marx and Lenin had supported the idea of compensation and, if necessary, paying very well. Lenin also had stated that 'only that power can be stable which avowedly and unconditionally rests upon the majority of the population'. Surely free democratic elections were the civilised way to settle this, I argued. This reasoning gave the material necessary to our people to justify their faith in the Labour Party methods. It was easy, of course, with the mass unemployment and the trickery tactics of the Tories at elections for communists to argue that reason could not succeed, but on the whole they began to build up, and more and more of the active elements threw themselves into the work of the Party.

The 1931 election had been a terrible blow to our people. Ramsay MacDonald and Snowden going off to the other side broke the hearts of many of the older socialists who also on this account dropped out of the movement. But perhaps the greater damage was done by Maxton and the ILP whose anti-Labour propaganda had confused our own people and weakened their enthusiasm. The people would have stood by the Labour Party against the Tories but they were distracted by this attack from within. Many of the ILP-ers who had remained attached to the Party of their youth were not prepared to follow Maxton into the wilderness and yet did not want to begin a new interest in the Labour Party. This all did immeasurable harm. The ILP also had another great advantage over the Labour Party in the form of its organisation. Its branches were enthusiastic individuals who worked together as a team, socially friendly, and with their interests centred in their branch. The Labour Party is a federal party, and when a constituency party meets, it is a group of delegates from branches of trades unions, local Labour parties and ward committees. The main power of the Labour Party is therefore exercised by delegates who have only a periodic association and little possibility of permanent or social association. The ILP was small and intimate. The Labour Party by its very size could not have this advantage. This was different in small towns and villages where groups could work in the old way, whatever they were called.

I was Secretary of the Scottish Council of the Labour Party for seven years till I went to Parliament in 1939. By then the Labour Party was firmly established. The SSP had dissolved and discipline had been inculcated so far as the Communist Party boring from within was concerned. The CP was always trying to permeate the Party and the rules were very definite against any collaboration by Labour Party members with the communists. On one occasion, some of the executive of the Dundee Trades and Labour Council had taken part in some communist demonstration. The Secretary John Muir phoned me up to find out what he should do. It would have been possible to have brought them before the local party and had a long wrangle for months about whether or not they should be expelled. I advised the Secretary to write to the six members concerned, telling them that since they had ceased to comply with the terms of membership laid down in the constitution they were no longer eligible as members of the party, and that he was sorry they had by their action left the party. They at once appealed to the Scottish Council on whose behalf I replied, saying that I also was sorry they had left the party but that we were all bound by the constitution we had accepted. I said I was sure, however, that if they desired to be in the party and did accept the constitution, there seemed to be no reason why they should not resume their membership. Upon which they expressed their regrets to the Secretary, resumed their membership and peace was restored before the party met.

The Dundee Trades and Labour Council felt all this happening outside their ken had diddled them of their authority in some way. I was asked to the party meeting, for, of course, to settle a matter of this kind without debate was unheard of. Since the Trades and Labour Council included as well as supporters of the Labour Party purely trades union delegates, not affiliated for Labour Party purposes, it was essential that these should not discuss Labour Party affairs. I therefore prepared a document setting out the essential parts of the constitution and instructed the Secretary not to allow anyone in who did not accept the constitution of the Labour Party. Out of about ninety-four delegates ninety signed the document and came in. I agreed to allow the other four in and they promptly raised the question as to why this had been done. I explained the constitution and then they also agreed to sign so they were all free to have a go at me, after which honour was satisfied.

The next morning the *Daily Worker* came out with a large headline – 'Woodburn's Black Circular'[13] – and this was followed later by an attack upon me by Stafford Cripps at a meeting in Falkirk. Following this, I issued a summary of the constitutional points for the acceptance of all candidates for local councils and Parliament since we had all sorts of trouble with people who got into office and then began to play the communist game. This new document caused another furore and the National Executive of the Labour Party was appealed to, but they could hardly object to my enforcing the conditions of the constitution. It is interesting that Krishna Menon,[14] who became the Foreign Secretary of India, when he was adopted for Dundee, had to sign on the dotted line. In later years, he was always very friendly in spite of his resentment at this iron discipline. The communists then tried to attack me through the Scottish Trades Union Congress. We had some joint conferences with the result that the STUC also had to lay down rules of procedure for its members on joint bodies.

The splits – personal and party – in Parliament were a great handicap to my work for they automatically communicated themselves to the localities. We had a series of organised sectional movements. Stafford Cripps and others had formed the Socialist League and were playing with the CP in united and 'popular' fronts. After the Spanish revolt, popular fronts were advocated with both communists and liberals, and it was quite difficult to keep our people from being swept away by these emotional movements largely sponsored by the Communist Party. I was, however, not prepared to enforce a discipline on the rank and file which did not apply to the leaders. So when Arthur Brady, a member of the Scottish Council, defied warnings and took the chair for a united front meeting with Harry Pollitt,[15] the Communist Party leader, I had to tell him that he also had left the Party by ceasing to comply with the conditions governing membership. The Scottish Council endorsed my action and that helped greatly in making our decisions respected.

In 1936 the Labour Party Conference met in Edinburgh. The only hall capable of holding it was the Usher Hall and there a vital change of policy was made. The Labour Party foreign policy was that of supporting collective security through the League of Nations. It

[13] *Daily Worker*, 29 May 1937. The *Daily Worker* was established in 1930 as the newspaper of the CPGB.

[14] Krishna Menon (1896–1974), politician and diplomat, pre-selected for Dundee in 1940, High Commissioner for India in London 1947–52, Indian Defence Minister 1957–62.

[15] Harry Pollitt (1890–1960), political organiser, founding member of CPGB and its secretary 1929–56.

had rejected unilateral disarmament. The Trades Unions – Ernest Bevin, Walter Citrine and others – had come back from the continent with information about Hitler's preparations for war. Yet many of our people refused to see the facts and there was great reluctance here, as in France, to face up to the dangers. The Spanish revolt, however, had helped to open people's eyes, and even Maxton, who was opposed to the Labour Party supporting defence policies, had said in Parliament 'if they ask me to go to Spain and fight, I will go to Spain'. There was, indeed, a demand from socialists to stand up to the dictators who were already destroying the trades union and labour movement on the continent. Spain brought home to the public the ruthless methods of Hitler and Mussolini, and the government were being denounced for not facing up to the menace. It seemed a little illogical that Maxton, who was in favour of standing up and fighting the dictators in Spain, was later prepared, in his own words on the Spanish issue, to support a policy of 'crawling in front of the fascist powers' when they attacked ourselves. In 1936, however, the Labour Party conference decided that 'the armed strength of the countries loyal to the league of nations must be conditioned by the armed strength of the potential aggressors'. When this vote was being announced, I was standing in the side aisle with Stafford Cripps and George Lansbury. The latter said to me 'I know that this is necessary but I am not the man to be responsible'. George also was more of a prophet than practical and felt himself frustrated by having to confine his ideals and evangel to the limits of practical politics.

Stafford Cripps at this time was actually advocating that 'every possible step should be made to stop recruiting for the armed forces' on the grounds that this would force the government to introduce conscription which would provide a better platform from which to attack them. I contested his view in the *Forward* and we had a controversy ranging over some weeks. At this time, he was opposing any support of the government in its rearmament. As it happened, I had a further controversy with Cripps in March of 1939 by which time he was pushing the idea of the popular front. In 1937 he had lined up with Maxton and Pollitt and, with other friends of the Socialist League, had severed with the Labour Party. We were now being asked to join up with all parties willing to combine against fascism. The snag was that this was simply the latest Communist Party stunt and their policy was liable to change as Russia's needs dictated, as was eventually demonstrated in 1939. On this occasion, Aneurin Bevan, feeling that Cripps was getting the worst of the debate, came into the columns of the *Forward* to reply to me in defence of Cripps.

There was and always will be a strong pacifist attitude in the Scottish Labour movement and it was difficult for us to make up our minds on this fascist and Nazi threat. It was necessary, therefore, to state the issues again and again, and for months there was a steady debate between myself and Emrys Hughes,[16] I representing the Labour Party official view and he the purely pacifist outlook. I could not follow his logic, which was, for example, in favour of the workers striking against sending material to dictators, which action might have been, in certain circumstances, declared by them to be an act of war, and refusing to face up to the consequences of having to defend the seamen who carried out the policy.

These public controversies were all incidental to the work of organising throughout Scotland – there were few parts of Scotland I did not touch in the process. I also had the job of supervising by-elections which usually meant being election agent. The first was the famous East Fife by-election with five candidates. Lord Beaverbrook[17] took part on behalf of the candidate he was supporting and later blamed this election for giving him the asthma which plagued him for the rest of his life. Joe Westwood[18] was the Labour candidate and gave us our first increased vote since 1931. Eric Linklater[19] made this election the basis of a novel, *Magnus Merriman*. Then we had a university by-election with Naomi Mitchison[20] as our candidate and a second one with Robert (later Lord) Gibson.[21] The latter took place when the Conservatives were split over India, Winston Churchill leading the rebels of that day. It was interesting that so strong was the feeling against the government, even a former Tory cabinet minister, Austen Chamberlain,[22] voted Labour! The election was on the proportional representation register and we saw all the votes. It was interesting to see how many lawyers and graduates had spoiled papers because they had forgotten to sign their names.

---

[16] Emrys Hughes (1894–1969), politician, MP for South Ayrshire 1946–69.
[17] William Maxwell Aitken, first Baron Beaverbrook (1879–1964), newspaper magnate and politician.
[18] Joseph Westwood (1884–1948), trade unionist and politician, organiser for the Scottish Miners' Union 1918–29, MP Peebles and South Midlothian 1922–31, Stirling and Falkirk District of Burghs 1935–48, Secretary of State for Scotland 1945–7. The East Fife by-election of 1933 had five candidates.
[19] Eric Robert Russell Linklater (1899–1974), writer, stood as a nationalist candidate at East Fife.
[20] Naomi Mary Margaret Mitchison, Lady Mitchison (1897–1999), writer and social activist.
[21] Robert Gibson, Lord Gibson (1886–1965), MP for Greenock 1936–41.
[22] Sir Joseph Austen Chamberlain (1863–1937), MP for Worcestershire Eastern 1892–1914, Birmingham West 1914–37.

In the general election of 1935, we put candidates up against Maxton, McGovern,[23] Campbell Stephen,[24] George Buchanan[25] and Jennie Lee,[26] who were defending their seats as ILP-ers. This was necessary as otherwise they would have spread themselves over the whole of Scotland losing us, perhaps, many seats. In the midst of the election, Oliver Baldwin[27] came to see me. He was very disturbed at this opposition to the ILP and said they wanted to work with the Labour Party. I said nothing would please me better if that were the case and I was prepared to go a long way to help. I realised that it would not be easy for them to come back into the party as if they were giving in. I therefore offered that, if Maxton would protect me by a private letter giving me the necessary assurances, I would invite them publicly to come in to the party again. This would have made it an act of grace on their part and the responsibility would have been mine. I said he would kill the fatted calf if this happened. I had, of course, no specific authority from the executive except that I knew if it were agreed to it would become a fact. Oliver Baldwin delivered the message but all that Maxton said was that the Labour Party had plenty of 'fatted calves' for returning prodigals. Cripps also had approached me to see whether there was any chance of healing the breach but there was no hope. James Maxton preferred the privileged position in Parliament of being the leader of a small party without responsibility.

This gave him a right to the front stage in every big debate. He spoke as one of the four leaders. He did not seek power or responsibility, which would have been a handicap to his oratory, and it was too much to expect that he would give up that eminence to take his part in a team on the Labour front bench. For, of course, his popularity was such that he would have automatically been elected to office once he was working as a colleague. In his role of leader of a fourth party he delivered what I regard as one of the two most charming speeches I ever heard in the House of Commons. The occasion was Speaker

[23] John McGovern (1887–1968), politician and ILP member, MP for Glasgow Shettleston 1930–59.
[24] Campbell Stephen (1884–1947), politician and ILP member, MP for Glasgow Camlachie 1922–31, 1935–47.
[25] George Buchanan (1890–1955), politician and ILP member, MP for Glasgow Gorbals 1922–48, pensions minister 1947–8.
[26] Janet Lee, Baroness Lee of Asheridge (1904–88), politician and ILP member, MP for Lanarkshire Northern 1929–31, Cannock 1945–70, Minister for the Arts 1964–70.
[27] Oliver Ridsdale Baldwin, 2nd Earl Baldwin of Bewdley (1899–1958), MP for Dudley 1929–35, Paisley 1945–7.

FitzRoy's[28] golden wedding. The other was one by Wedgwood Benn on the Speaker's procession.

[The seven years I spent building the Labour Party to replace the ILP as the individual agency for membership was one of the busiest periods of my life. I was at it from early morning till late at night for usually seven days a week. My office was in the Gorbals, Glasgow, in what had been the elegant flat of citizens long since departed. It had plenty of daylight. I had a secretary who was modest but efficient. All I needed to do was to decide what was to be said and she would write splendid letters. Or, I wrote material out in shorthand and she transcribed it perfectly. In the South Edinburgh election, I had a secretary who, when she could not read her own shorthand, just typed what she thought it might be and it was more trouble deleting mistakes when they were plausibly and well composed. One of my main problems in keeping the party going smoothly was the tendency for disputes to arise. Parties would object to what councillors did, or either or both had conflicts over policy or rules, and in my earlier days much time was spend pouring oil on troubled waters or in laying down the law.

Once a party of Scots fell out about the interpretation of rules or policy, such an argument brought all work to a stop. An illustration of this was I was present at a meeting of Dundee Trades and Labour Council. When I was called at 9pm to speak, I said I was interested in how they used the time of the meeting. They had spent over half an hour arguing as to whether the meeting finished at 10pm on the clock on the wall or the time on the chairman's watch. The importance was that no decisions could be taken after 10[pm]. They then had spent ten minutes adopting candidates for their elections and then no time at all discussing how to get them elected. But the legal point had to be settled. One of the services I did was to decide many such issues for parties, and then they got on with the work. Such a waste of time as I have illustrated takes place in more important meetings. It is amazing how important business can be held up for long periods in the House of Commons on 'points of order' of no more importance than the Dundee closure time.]

A by-election took place at Dumfries where John Downie, a cooperative candidate, was the Labour candidate. Duncan Howie, the Cooperative Party organiser, acted as agent and I took charge of the political and publicity side. We usually decided in the morning what the publicity side of the speeches was to be, for in such a scattered

---

[28] Edward Algernon FitzRoy (1869–1943), Speaker of the House of Commons 1928–43.

area it was impossible for the press without great trouble to cover the meetings so late and catch the papers for the morning. So we had a press meeting in the morning and I dictated to the typist and the press at the same time the main gist of the report for the evening's speeches, subject, of course, to what the candidate actually said. Sir Harry Fildes[29] had made some slighting reference to Mr Downie's position as a civil service pensioner and the proposed report read somewhat as follows:

> Mr Downie expressed his regret that Sir Harry had lowered the tone of the election by introducing personalities in the form of references to the source of Mr Downie's income. Nevertheless since this had been done Mr Downie said he thought the people should know where a candidate got his income. He desired to make clear therefore that he, Mr Downie, got no money from profiteering in armament shares, he had no income the drink trade etc.

When I arrived the next morning, the press men were waiting for me in great excitement. They told me that Mr Downie had gone further than the line in his notes and asserted that the Tory Party got its funds from arms profiteering and the drink trade. Sir Harry Fildes was so angry that he had challenged Mr Downie and had offered £50 to the Dumfries Royal Infirmary if Mr Downie could prove that they did. The press asked me what Mr Downie would do. I said he would be prepared to give £50 to Dumfries infirmary if Sir Harry Fildes could prove that they did not. I heard no more about it.

Perhaps the most dramatic by-election I took part in was the one in Ross and Cromarty at the beginning of 1936. It was said to have been the press story of the century. It was necessary to find a good candidate and I proposed Hector McNeil[30] who had just had a spectacular result in Kelvingrove, where Walter Elliot was finally returned after many counts at a most unsatisfactory election. All sorts of irregularities had occurred. A presiding officer had got drunk and the affairs in his station were out of order. After the original count, other boxes were found and the result seemed to change from Hector to Walter with each new count. The counters refused to count any more unless they were given extra money and at one time, someone sent out to me for a copy of the Representation of the People Act to settle some dispute.

---

[29] Sir Henry Fildes (1870–1948), politician, MP for Stockport 1920–3, Dumfriesshire 1935–45.
[30] Hector McNeil (1907–55), politician, MP for Greenock 1941–55, Secretary of State for Scotland 1950–1.

So Hector was well known. He was a highlander and had a pleasant manner and appearance and was an able speaker.

The other candidates were Malcolm MacDonald,[31] the National candidate, Dr Russell Thomas,[32] the Liberal, and Randolph Churchill,[33] Independent Unionist. The election was further enlivened by visits to Dingwall of Fascists dressed in their black shirts, and a campaign of personal antagonism carried on by Lady Houston[34] against Malcolm MacDonald. We started the election in January 1936. Malcolm MacDonald had lost his seat at the election, as did his father at Seaham Harbour. His father had been adopted by the Scottish Universities and a seat was being found for Malcolm at Ross and Cromarty. The sons of two ex-ministers – one an ex-Prime Minister and the other a Prime Minister to be – heightened the interest and the election was covered by nearly all the lobby correspondents. No sooner had the election got under way than we were involved in one of the worst winters the area has had. Malcolm Macmillan[35] went with me to the west coast and we found ourselves blocked by snow, in danger of sliding off roads. The telephone lines were down and our headquarters at Dingwall had no idea where we were. Hector McNeil's car was charged by a stag one night and in evading it they nearly went over the hillside.

We had one specially bad night on the Black Isle. Hector was speaking at Cromarty and I had to follow on from Conon Bridge. It was a terrific blizzard and it was almost impossible to see through the wall of snow. I kept to the side of the road not knowing there was a deep ditch running alongside the hedge and my car sank gently down to its axle. We tried to dig it out. Another car came along which happened to be taking Randolph Churchill back to Dingwall and he gallantly stopped and with a rope attached to his car, tried to drag us back on to the road. It was of no use. I had to tramp about a half mile along the road in the blizzard to phone to Dingwall to send out a crane, which they did.

When we got back to Dingwall, we learned that the King was dying and we listened to Sir John Reith's[36] impressive announcement. This

---

[31]   Malcolm John MacDonald (1901–81), politician and diplomat, son of Ramsay MacDonald, MP for Nottinghamshire Bassetlaw 1929–35, Ross and Cromarty 1936–45, Secretary of State for Dominion Affairs and for the Colonies 1935–40, Minister for Health 1940–1.

[32]   William Stanley Russell Thomas (1896–1957), politician, MP for Southampton 1940–5.

[33]   Randolph Frederick Edward Spencer Churchill (1911–68), journalist and politician, son of Winston Churchill, MP for Preston 1940–5.

[34]   Dame Fanny Lucy Houston (1857–1936), financial adventuress.

[35]   Malcolm Macmillan (1913–78), politician, MP for the Western Isles 1935–70.

[36]   John Charles Walsham Reith, first Baron Reith (1889–1971), first Director-Gener-

raised a new issue – what was to happen to the election? Meantime, there was no news of Hector McNeil coming back. My wife had just returned after their car had been embedded in snowdrifts and rescued by a farmer with his horses. So we had to organise a search party for the candidate. One of the garage proprietors offered to take his car which he said was equipped with automatic jacks. These were helpful on such occasions and he also knew the roads. Off we went. We found the road to Cromarty blocked so we made up over the hill and after charging through some small drifts the car got itself solidly buried in another. We had spades and it took us from 10 o'clock till midnight to get ourselves extricated. Meantime, we could see the tops of cars just peeping through deeper drifts further down the road so we turned back and made for Dingwall. There we were told that Hector McNeil had returned two hours ago and had gone to take a hot bath, since when he had not been seen. As we were to have a conference immediately in the Queen's Hotel about the king's death, we had to find him. He was fast asleep in the bath. A truce was arranged and on the following morning we all attended one of the most curious memorial services ever held where all the normally irreconcilable churches were represented.

One night, we were coming back from the Gairloch when our car, which was going quite slow, suddenly wheeled round on the ice and struck a telegraph pole. This saved us all, for otherwise we would have gone over a steep embankment. I used the jack to force the car back off the pole, which was wedged between the bonnet and the mudguard, and we were able to proceed. Going down the hill on the ice, it looked again as if we were going to miss the bridge and plunge into the burn when the car took an equally erratic turn and swept us on to the bridge. John Carvel[37] of the *Daily Express* got a bad fright when his car seemed to be making for the edge of the ravine of the Rogie Falls when it fortunately righted itself and reached home safely. The press men thought it was wiser after that to keep at the end of the trunk telephone line to London. The *Daily Express* was worried when it was discovered that all their scoops were being scooped. There was a veteran reporter in Dingwall attached, I think, to the *Ross-Shire Journal* and evidently, he had a grape vine which collected all the *Express* reports as they went out. After that, a special wire was laid into the hotel for their use.

Probably no election had had such a galaxy of speaking talent. Being in the parliamentary recess and the candidates being who they were, it was indeed a fight of gladiators. It was interesting that the four

al of the BBC.

[37] John Lees Carvel (d. 1959), sub-editor of the *Scottish Daily Express* and author of books about Scotland under the pseudonym Ian C. Lees.

candidates and myself all were finally MPs in the same Parliament. Malcolm MacDonald was the Dominions Secretary and in the early part of the war I heard him winding up a debate with a truly magnificent speech. Not long afterwards, he was appointed High Commissioner to Canada and has since shown great wisdom in several semi-diplomatic appointments.

In two of these by-elections, we had international crises – I think it was during the Dumfries and the South Ayrshire elections – and in both cases I had to improvise Labour's policy since the candidate was expected to pronounce on them without waiting to consult the leaders – candidates are supposed both to speak for themselves and to commit the party. Once [was] when Mussolini invaded Abyssinnia and the other was his attack on Albania. Our policy was that of the League of Nations – to apply economic boycotts to the aggressor and any other means necessary to restrain him and if necessary stop him. Asked if that meant war, our candidate explained that, when a policeman restrained a fighting drunk, that was not war – it was police action. George Lansbury at Dumfries was challenged about this policy and replied that he was in favour of a small international police force. Of course, a police force needs to be of a size capable of doing the job.

During all that period, Labour had never lost a by-election and in Scotland, our vote had gone steadily up. With Robert Gibson we won Greenock for the first time. There, at least, our election machine on the Labour side worked like a Rolls Royce, though I was plagued all the time by a civil war between Provost Bell and Councillor Mrs McLeod over a slander action. However they both worked loyally under me for the election.

Mr Attlee had promised to help a candidate who was adopted for Ross and Cromarty and we made his visit the occasion for a tour through the Highland constituencies. I had known him quite well in the course of my job and during this fortnight we shared meetings in many places and picnicked on our day time journeys in various beauty spots. Mrs Attlee, my wife and a young cousin who was over from France did the cooking and buying, and we had a pleasant time with some excellent meetings in the evenings. We took turnabout with home and foreign policy and I discovered then what was more apparent to me later when together in government, that our minds seemed to see problems and solutions in much the same way. Perhaps for this reason I have always thought he had one of the clearest minds in British politics. He was and is a difficult conversationalist. He has no small talk. His comments are almost telegrammatic and yet read like epigrams. I cannot think of anyone who can say so much in so few words. He used to present problems to the Party for their consideration and judgement. By the time he sat down there was little to be added which contributed to understanding.

He was a different man in the bosom of his family, which was nearer to his heart than politics, and it was not any personal ambition which made him Prime Minister. Chance played a big part. The 1931 election had left us few MPs on the Labour benches and when George Lansbury was made leader, the likely choice for deputy was Stafford Cripps. But he had not been ready to give up his practice at the Bar and Mr Attlee was made deputy. On the eve of Stafford Cripps' expulsion from the Party at a later time, we were staying together in a hotel in Dundee where we were speaking at a conference the following day. He felt rather bitter about what seemed the ingratitude of the movement for all he had done. He referred to this question of the leadership and he was under the impression that Mr Attlee had become the deputy merely as a temporary tenant of the position until it suited Stafford's convenience to take on the job. He felt somehow that he had been let down.

How far this idea in his mind contributed to his proving for a time so awkward a colleague is anyone's guess. I told him that his difficulty was that he had come into the Labour Party at the top and had never got to know the mind of the people who ran it – the secretaries, the branch members, and so on. Lloyd George once said he never feared the leaders of the socialists – it was their lance corporals who to him seemed formidable. I explained to Stafford how the workers liked him and thought him a great chap, but they really were afraid of him as a leader. He had all the courage of those who were accustomed to taking risks. The workers normally had only a week or two between them and starvation, and they liked to know where they were going. Stafford's policies, I said, were too variable and shook their confidence, especially when they so often varied according to the persons he was making his intimate friends at the time. Some of these were leading communists.

This I believe to be the weakness of barristers as political leaders. They have become so accustomed to speaking from briefs that they seldom have clear policy of their own. I often thought that Stafford's later practice of inviting working men MPs to his house, where informal minutes were taken of the conversations, were his attempt to get into the mind of the rank and file. Although I opposed his, to me, irrational policies, we always remained good friends. He was a remarkable man with a remarkable brain. He could grasp a subject and make it his own with such conviction that he convinced people almost against their better judgement. He was capable of great errors of judgement, as when leader of the House under Mr Churchill he lectured the members on their absence from the chamber without having first ascertained that they were nearly all attending a special meeting upstairs to meet the members of English local authorities to discuss legislation coming before the House.

He had recently returned from Moscow where he had been ambassador. He was not then a member of the Labour Party, not having been yet readmitted after his expulsion. He had great confidence in his schemes and himself as their agent and had proposed that he go to Moscow and try and come to terms with Russia. He had a thin time. Stalin never even received him till Lord Beaverbrook and Harriman[38] went, and when Stafford returned to this country he was of [the] opinion that if Russia were attacked, it would not last a fortnight. On the way out of Russia he had invited all the officials at Murmansk to a dinner but one after the other declined. At a small dinner, he told us how he almost always had to sit beside the same young woman at functions and could get little communication with Russians of consequence. All this changed when Russia came into the war, and on Stafford's return to Russia, he was more friendlily received. When Stafford came back, finally everyone was convinced that he had brought Russia in on our side. So great was his reputation that he was talked of as the successor to Winston who everyone thought would topple soon from his throne.

Conservatives asked me what our people thought. My view was that Anthony Eden[39] would succeed him. Shortly afterwards, Cripps went to the Ministry of Aircraft Production and ceased to be Leader of the House. Whatever the reasons for the shift – and of them I have no knowledge – he did a wonderful job in that ministry. He knew the value, as does Winston Churchill, of dramatising power and when he visited a factory or called a conference, it was staged magnificently. Manufacturers and others ate out of his hand. He had ideas in the execution of a job and I have seen industrialists simply on his instructions give orders to build a factory here or there. The redevelopment of our industry owes a lot to his drive and leadership. During a great deal of this time he was completely independent in politics. As leader of the House he had a Parliamentary Private Secretary from both the Labour and Tory sides of the House.

This young cousin from France I referred to was about sixteen or seventeen. She had the opportunity of seeing Scotland in a way not open to many, for if my duties involved an interesting journey, my wife and Maud came along. One of the most unusual duties I had at that time was to represent our leaders at the funeral of the earl of

---

[38] W. Averell Harriman (1891–1986), American politician, businessman and diplomat. The Harriman-Beaverbrook mission of September 1941 to discuss large-scale aid.

[39] Robert Anthony Eden, first earl of Avon (1897–1977), politician, MP for Warwick and Leamington 1923–57, Prime Minister 1955–7.

Kinnoull.[40] He was a curious little man with the record of a hectic youth. He had married the daughter of Mrs Merrick, a rather famous nightclub hostess. I first met him at a meeting in the Caird Hall, Dundee, where I was speaking with Arthur Greenwood. Suddenly, there appeared in the anteroom a wizened little man, with a shabby morning coat and a bowler hat. At first glance I thought it was Arthur Greenwood's cabman coming for his fare. He was a pathetic but now earnest person who had found a new purpose in life by joining the Labour Party. He had a small car with an outside dicky seat. Leaving a Kilsyth meeting, we were to be taken to Falkirk station. It was a cold frosty night and Arthur Greenwood and I had to decide who would sit on Lady Kinnoul's lap in the front seat and who would shiver on the dicky. I chose the dicky for Arthur was on friendly terms with both of them. The Lady was luxuriously upholstered in a quilted fashion, pleasant and kindly, but I should not think interested in politics.

The little man died shortly afterwards and was to be buried in the family burial ground on the estate near Perth. It was the loneliest funeral I've ever attended. It was outside the estate wall and it was surrounded on the other three sides by extensive fields. James Welsh MP,[41] the author of poems and novels of the mines, represented the parliamentary party. Lady Kinnoull and her brother and I think the gravedigger completed, with us, the mourners. It was a lonely and queer end for the 14th earl of a Scottish noble house.

[40]   George Harley Hay, 14th earl of Kinnoull (1902–38), politician, entered the House of Lords as a Conservative but joined the Labour Party in 1930.
[41]   James C. Welsh (1880–1954), trade unionist, politician and writer, MP for Coatbridge 1922–31, Bothwell 1935–45.

CHAPTER SEVEN

I had had to give up the right to stand for Parliament when I became Scottish Secretary of the Labour Party since I was responsible for the selection of candidates. Wedgwood Benn and other of my friends in Parliament had been pressing me to stand. They thought that I had done the job I started out to do and that I ought to be in the Commons. I must confess that the trouble I had over all the splits and quarrels of the time in the Commons had rather made me feel well out of it and I had ceased to think about it. When Lauchlan MacNeill Weir[1] died in 1939, however, it was suggested that I should consider allowing my name to go forward. The chairman of the constituency party was of the opinion that the seat should be utilised for a leading member of the movement and he kindly thought of me in that connection.

Although I was not obliged by the terms of my engagement so to do, I decided that it would not be possible to do so without first resigning from my post. After talking it over with my wife and prominent members of the party, I sent in my resignation and allowed my name to go forward. There was no guarantee that I would be successful as there was a member of the National Executive and an official candidate of the largest trade union in Britain – of which I was also a member – anxious for a seat and many others ready to offer. In accordance with my usual custom, I gave the party a list of all who were available. Dick Windle,[2] the Assistant National Agent, took over the duties of supervision since I was involved. There were five nominees who finally came before the selection conference and I was selected by a clear majority at the first vote. What pleased me most of all was that the other unselected candidates were the finest workers I had in the election which followed and they remained my friends all through the years I have been in Parliament.

[1] Lauchlan MacNeill Weir (1877–1939), writer and politician, MP for Clackmannan and Eastern Stirlingshire, 1922–31, 1935–39.
[2] Richard T. Windle (1888–1951), Labour Party Assistant National Agent 1929–46, National Agent 1946–51.

When the proceedings for the election started, it was expected that we should have to fight it in the normal way. While it seemed a safe Labour seat, actually it had only once been held by a clear majority over the other candidates – of only thirty-four. But as the selection procedures developed we came nearer and nearer to war and actually my selection conference was held two hours after war was declared on 3 September 1939. We had had an air raid warning in Edinburgh that morning and there was word of no one being able to travel. However I had been roped in to assist in the public relations side and I had enough official status to take me to Larbert in case of difficulty. In view of the war, a party truce was declared and it looked as if I would have an uncontested return, but a pacifist candidate stood with the support of the ILP and backed financially by the marquis of Tavistock.[3] The Communist Party at that time were in favour of the war as a resistance to fascism but before the end of my election, the Molotov pact had been signed by Russia with Hitler and the CP had changed round to the war. The communist readjustment, however, was in the transition stage during the election and so far as they were concerned we were left alone.

James Maxton came up to speak, but before he got there, we had issued a small newspaper in which he was quoted as being willing to fight fascism in Spain and he found himself having to answer why he was not prepared to do as much when Britain itself was involved. He was annoyed and explained that he had got to know me in prison, presumably thinking this would have a damaging effect on the result. There was a small poll but a large majority. I expect a good many conservatives simply did not vote. I got 15,645 and Stewart[4] 1,060. The election was 13 October 1939.

I was at the office on Monday the 16th and was coming through from Glasgow when we saw a commotion in the sky. We did not realise what was happening but when we got to Edinburgh, we discovered we had been seeing the first air raid of the war. The people had been out in the streets watching what looked like puffs of cotton wool in the sky, little realising that these were explosions and that bullets were flying about. A painter was struck while painting a window. The Lord Provost's house in Portobello was shot up. I left that night for London to take my seat and I left full of the local indignation about the air raid. Fifteen planes had come over and everyone was indignant that only seven had been shot down. Such innocence in view of our

---

[3]   Hastings William Sackville Russell, 12th duke of Bedford (1888–1953), evangelical Christian and pacifist.
[4]   Andrew Stewart, assistant editor of *Peace News*, which had launched in 1936 and reached peak circulation (c. 40,000) around the time of Woodburn's by-election.

later experiences! However, after I had been introduced I told Neil McLean[5] about the raid and the strong feeling. He advised me to put down a question to the Prime Minister for answer on the Thursday. I caused a great laugh, however, the second day I was there when Capt. Wallace[6] was answering questions on whether he would establish a National Transport Board to ensure vital services. He explained how negotiations were taking place between the road and rail interests and I put a supplementary question, 'Does the Rt. Hon. Gentleman agree that the national interests should come before either road or rail interests?', which was greeted with good natured laughter. It was quick work for a new member. When I look back, it must have been considered an unprecedented presumption on the part of a new member but it was quite innocently done. This applied to my question to Mr Chamberlain:

> Mr Woodburn to ask the Secretary of State for Air (to whom the question had been transferred) whether he will cause inquiry to be made to ascertain how enemy aircraft were able to reach the Forth Bridge without apparent challenge and how those aircraft which escaped from the attack of the local anti-aircraft defences were able to reach the open sea again nearly forty miles from the scene of the fighting without interruption.

None of us fully appreciated what a tremendous success had been achieved by the 'amateurs' who went up from Turnhouse and brought nearly fifty per cent of the raiders down. I became familiar with the atmosphere of the House by asking questions and on 1 November, I delivered my maiden speech on the question of the old age pensions. I notice that one of the early questions I asked was about the location of industry and the danger to Scotland of being based so much on heavy industry and the probability of this bringing unemployment when peace came.

My speech on old age pensions was the first of several attempts I made to get pensions placed on a rational basis. I wanted all the sordid business of humiliating old people by means tests to be done away with by the introduction of a scheme where people could pay for the right to a pension, which I said we were all quite willing to do. The Chancellor of the Exchequer, Sir John Simon,[7] followed me and after

---

[5] Neil Maclean (1873–1953), politician, MP for Glasgow Govan 1918–50.
[6] David Euan Wallace (1892–1941), army officer and politician, Conservative MP for Rugby 1922–3, Hornsey 1923–41, Minister of Transport 1939–40.
[7] John Allsebrook Simon, first Viscount Simon (1873–1954), politician and lawyer, Liberal MP for Walthamstow 1906–18, Spen Valley 1922–40, Home Secre-

some complimentary remarks he took up the suggestion I had made and discussed its possibility. It was not long till such a scheme was introduced. My next speech was on the question of the cost of raising loans and inflation. I soon entered into what was then a small and select company – those who discussed finance.

Perhaps I could here digress a little and summarise how circumstances had equipped me to take at least an intelligent part in a great range of political affairs. I had the working-class and trade union atmosphere in which I had lived my early life. I had the experience of running the small family business with all its trials and tribulation. I had had twenty-five years' experience of engineering and iron founding, being concerned with shipping, international trade, settlement of accounts by foreign bills, correspondence in three or four languages, and in estimating and costing, had been involved in the practical economics of industry. The business was also reasonably small so that one got experience of nearly every problem to a greater or smaller degree. I had spent nearly twenty years studying and lecturing on economics, finance, history, anthropology and many other subjects and my experience of the first world war caused me to make myself familiar with secret diplomacy and the problems of war and peace. I had been for seven years Secretary of the Labour Party in Scotland and knew the country from end to end and a great many people. I had had to draft policy statements for Scotland and for the party as a whole, and I had had to understand and explain to our members all the party was doing in Parliament.

When Philip Snowden set up the Macmillan Committee after the 1929 conference at Brighton, where I had contested the accepted ideas about the solution of the financial crisis, I elected to give evidence. So far as I could see, nearly all those who were going to appear from the trades union or socialist side were going to discuss 'control of wholesale prices' and other such temporary treatments. No one, it appeared, was going to discuss the fundamental of the whole problem. Here was a committee established by a socialist Chancellor whose party held it had the cure for the evils of capitalism in socialism, and yet no one was going to say how socialism would tackle this problem of finance and industry.

I drew up my evidence which consisted of an analysis of the reasons for the booms and slumps which had dislocated society from time to time over the last century: this could be cured only by a planned control over progress. We were in a transition stage between private enterprise

tary 1915–16, 1935–7, Foreign Secretary 1931–5, Chancellor of the Exchequer 1937–40, Lord Chancellor 1940–5.

and public enterprise, and private enterprise was periodically breaking down because it could not find markets for all it could produce. At one time there was overproduction relative to the markets and at others there was underproduction. Together these made the swing of the pendulum violent and disturbing to economic life.

We had to recognise what was happening and the government must accept the role of the governor on the steam engine which keeps the speed steady, reducing it when it advances and accelerating it when it slows down. This was, I proposed, to be done by the use of credit for public purposes. When private enterprise was showing signs of recession, the government should advance credit for the development of public enterprise. But this, I pointed out, would immediately stimulate private enterprise, and if both went on together it would cause inflation. At this point the government should contract public enterprise and allow private enterprise to expand until it was necessary for public enterprise once again to fill the gap. In this way I suggested we would get a peaceful and uneventful evolution from capitalism into socialism. I dealt a good deal with the use of credit and when inflation occurred. This all seems very familiar today but to the best of my knowledge, that was the first time this theory was advanced. Cecil Lubbock[8] of the Bank of England and son of Lord Avebury jokingly told me afterwards that if he were in Edinburgh, he would attend my classes. The most important listener for my purposes was J.M. Keynes[9] and a year or two later he published a much talked of treatise, the substance of which was the theory I advanced to the Macmillan Committee.

After the war broke out and the Commonwealth prime ministers started to come to this country, the Labour Party in Parliament gave a reception to John Curtin,[10] the Prime Minister of Australia. When I went in, he was talking to Hugh Dalton who introduced me. John Curtin immediately said, 'but I know Mr Woodburn very well. It was on the basis of his teaching that we founded the financial policy of the Australian Labour Party and Government.' In the speech he delivered later to Labour Party MPs he repeated this when telling of the development of the Labour Party in Australia. No one was more astonished than I was.

But I still have the letter I received from the Australian Labour Party in 1932 which said they had been studying my *Outline of Finance* and my evidence before the Macmillan Committee and they wrote to me because a great many people in Australia has been attracted by

8   Cecil Lubbock (1872–1956), was a director of the Bank of England for thirty-two years and deputy governor 1923–5.
9   John Maynard Keynes, Baron Keynes (1883–1946), economist.
10 John Curtin (1885–1945), journalist and Prime Minister of Australia 1941–5.

the theories of Major Douglas.[11] They had been in communication 'with seven so-called economists, men who are supposed to devote their time to the teaching of economics, and the result was in every case either an evasion of the question or an admission of ignorance of Major Douglas' proposals'. He said the result of his appeal to them for guidance was nil. As it happened, I had been overwhelmed at home here by being asked for reviews of the voluminous literature which poured out on the Douglas scheme and was involved in debates. I was able therefore to send them an analysis of the theory and show what was good and what was bad in it. So far as it was practicable, it was neither more nor less than an intelligent use of credit by the government on the lines that the banking system had used credit for generations. It was both big and generous of Mr Curtin and was a surprise to many of my own colleagues.

Before I resume the subject of my life in Parliament, there is one more incident which ought to be mentioned. In 1934 Arthur Henderson, Secretary of the Labour Party, died and I was asked by the National Union of Railwaymen to allow my name to be put forward as his successor. I took the view that it was the duty of everyone to be ready to serve if he was the right person, though I had no great ambition to leave Scotland. I was placed on the short leet and in the final vote, J.S. Middleton,[12] the existing Assistant Secretary, was elected over me by thirteen votes to eleven. I had done nothing to push my claims and Ellen Wilkinson, who was on the Executive, was very wroth that I had not let her know. She said she could have turned the scales. I still adhered to my view that the Executive had the duty to pick the best person and it was up to them to decide. On a later occasion, after I was in Parliament, I was again asked but I declined for by that time I had had my fill of organisation.

I soon found in Parliament that one had to specialise and I was quite pleased to apply myself to financial and economic problems and was prominent in the debates on such subjects right up till I became a member of the government in 1945.

My predecessor as MP for Clackmannan had been Lachlan McNeil Weir. He had always been rather caustic in his comments on Parliament, both in the press and in the party meetings. I used to find it rather depressing when I was at his meetings as Scottish Secretary. So at the end of a year, in my first report, I gave my local party some idea of what a private MP could do.

[11] Clifford High Douglas (1879–1952), economic theorist and pioneer of social credit.
[12] James Smith Middleton (1878–1962), Labour Party Assistant Secretary 1902–34, Secretary 1934–44.

Question time is a very important part of parliamentary proceedings and many reforms are carried through as the result of prompting in such questions. As the result of a letter I received, I put down a question of the desirability of having news broadcast in Gaelic and this was agreed to. When I hear people grumbling about the interruption to their programmes in English, I keep it dark that I started it all. Some may be important though simple reforms, as when I got permission for the soldiers to have open-necked tunics when off duty. Such cases include a speech and question which gave rise to pay-as-you-earn. When I gave just a simple list of what a private MP could do from the back benches, my workers had a different feeling about Parliament.

Some questions have considerable human interest. An Edinburgh doctor who was in charge of a mental home brought to my notice that every discharged soldier-patient had a letter sent to his relatives saying he might become dangerous. I took the matter up with Oliver Stanley[13] who at first defended it but later made the War Office send out a letter of apology to all the families who had got the letters. Another simple but to my mind important achievement was the insertion of payment through the post office for supplementary pensions which everyone now takes for granted. In foreign affairs I spoke a good deal against the policy of strengthening the Germans by leaving unanswered the propaganda that Britain was out to destroy the German people – what later became the unconditional surrender policy. I was opposing this as far back as 1940.

Almost at the beginning of the war, I was appointed a member of the Select Committee on National Expenditure. This was considered a great honour for a young MP but it was a most interesting job in connection with the war. We examined into all possible sources of waste and divided ourselves at first into sub-committees to watch over certain departments. I became a member of the sub–committee which dealt with the Ministry of Supply under the chairmanship of Sir Herbert Williams.[14] He was a self-made man, an engineer and a rough diamond. He was a director of many companies and was an expert on House of Commons procedure. He was ruthless in his examination of witnesses. He examined all the ministry witnesses as if they were prisoners at the bar. I used to ask them leading questions from my practical experience which allowed them to

[13] Oliver Frederick George Stanley (1896–1950), Conservative MP for Westmoreland 1924–45, Bristol West 1945–50, Minister of Labour 1934–5, President of the Board of Trade 1937–40, Secretary of State for war 1940, Colonial Secretary 1942–5.
[14] Herbert Williams (1884–1954), Conservative MP for Reading 1924–9, Croydon South 1932–45, Croydon East 1950–4.

give the reasonable explanation. Admiral Brown,[15] who was responsible to the Cabinet for the technical side, told me that about a year before the war he had been told by the Prime Minister to organise production on the basis of an armed force of about 500,000: when in 1939 it was seen that France was going to collapse, this was suddenly stepped up to 5,000,000. It did not need much practical experience to understand the technical difficulties such a decision involved and I did my best to see that the witnesses were not made the culprit and bullied for a change in policy for which they had no responsibility.

My connection with foundries was responsible for changing the direction of the committee's activities almost at the start. A firm in my constituency wrote me that they had been asked to tender for stoves but that the specification was so drawn that only one firm could quote. I saw that this type of specification could give the firm to whom it applied a monopoly and on investigation of this particular case, we discovered that there was something fishy and disciplinary action was taken. We also discovered, however, that in other cases also – such as machine tools – the specification of one leading firm had simply been copied and sent out to others. We immediately reported on the matter and it was made possible for all firms to tender for what fitted the need. But I suggested also that the greatest waste was not that of money – it was the waste of manpower by inefficient production and it was agreed that this was our main purpose – to check wasteful specifications which by too elaborate demands caused a loss in production. Our activities in this connection must have saved millions of man hours. It was not only what we did but the committee's reputation was such that our very existence made every department and contractor watchful about economies. We discovered in this search many more examples. The War Office had some brilliant gentlemen who thought they should always have something better than the ordinary civilian. So, for example, when nearly all the patterns in the court were for five foot baths, he joyfully specified so many six foot. There were many such instances.

While our committee proceedings were secret, we did not think this should be interpreted in such a way as to keep valuable information we discovered from the departments. Sometimes we told the ministers privately. At other times in cross-examination we asked departmental witnesses 'are you aware that …?' and that made them aware. At the request of the Prime Minister we had to make a special investigation into the production of the Bofors gun.[16] When France collapsed and

---

[15] Andrew Browne Cunninghame, Viscount Cunningham of Hyndhope (1883–1963), naval officer.
[16] 40mm anti-aircraft autocannon developed by Swedish arms company AB Bofors.

we were faced with air raids, the defence people started asking where is the Bofors Gun. No one knew. The War Office could not trace it. As responsibility had gone over to the Ministry of Supply, our committee was asked to investigate. We discovered that the centre of operations was Birmingham and for the first time in the history of Parliament, a select committee left the precincts. Herbert Williams had some of Winston Churchill's qualities of cutting red tape.

When we got to Birmingham we could not start because the official reporter had lost the way, so I volunteered to take notes till he arrived. My knowledge of shorthand came in handy. The man responsible was a Swede or Dutchman in Morris Motors and when we got him before us to investigate the hold-up, we learned he was waiting for some special steel. We brought the steel maker and he said this steel had a low priority and he could not make it without stopping the rest. We asked him how many different steels he was making. The number was, I think, over forty. In answer to a question, he assured me that in many cases the same steel would do. As a result of our report, the varieties of these steel specification were reduced to about sixteen.

We found another very large firm had not been accustomed to working in millimetre sizes and was actually making the thickness of the firing platform to the nearest inch and then machining it down to the millimetre size – weakening it to comply with a size. The drawings had never been converted to inches. We did not wait to report to the House of Commons but returned to London and, by our usual method, got the ministry to shake the whole thing up. We also found in other guns spit and polish specifications greatly reducing output.

As the committee went on during the war, we changed the arrangements and committees were set up for ad hoc purposes. I became chairman of a sub-committee on finance and establishments. This was after my own heart and I proposed as our first investigation to find out how we borrowed for the war and what it cost. We arranged for Sir Reginald McKenna,[17] who had made a lot of speeches on the subject, and also for the Treasury to send witnesses. But the Treasury were for none of it and they claimed that we were exceeding our terms of reference, which did not include the consolidated fund. We could have gone to the House and asked for additional powers but recognised that if the Prime Minister was against it we would be defeated, so I accepted the compromise by which the Treasury proposed that they would give evidence provided we did not report on it. Sir Richard

---

[17] Reginald McKenna (1863–1943), politician and banker, Liberal MP for Monmouthshire Northern 1895–1918, First Lord of the Admiralty 1908–11, Home Secretary 1911–15, Chancellor of the Exchequer 1915–16.

Hopkins[18] came and gave evidence and I was able to cross-examine him on the waste that could be [prevented] if money was borrowed in one way rather than another. I was really also putting forward by my own questions – my own views that this country could not stand what was done after the first world war when Treasury bills and short-time cheap borrowing was converted into Treasury bonds at high rates of interest. From the answers, I am sure that the discussion had some effect in shaping the post-war policy of the Treasury.

The best job I did there, however, was in connection with organisation and methods. I was impressed by what the Organisation and Methods Department of the Treasury had been able to do, short circuiting all kinds of wasteful procedure. In our inquiries we examined business experts from outside as well as experts from the Treasury. Our most interesting witness perhaps was Sir Horace Wilson,[19] famous as the man who had accompanied Mr Chamberlain to Munich. He was at first a little inflexible but I finally got him to cooperate and he was very helpful. I asked him at the end if he would agree to answer a curiosity question. He had been reputed to be the man who had guided Mr Chamberlain and his policy in his Munich days – was this true? He replied that anyone who knew Mr Chamberlain would know that he decided his own policy. This view was confirmed later by Lord Strang[20] in his memoirs.

When it came to drafting reports this was usually first done by the secretary. Sir George Tomlinson,[21] who was acting in this capacity for us, was keen on curbing the Treasury and knew the history of the other ministries' struggle to keep their independence. In compiling our report, we made a division of labour, for I was anxious to bring out strongly our recommendation on organisation and methods. So I did this part and Sir George did the Treasury history. This report was the only one so far as I know which went through both the sub-committee and the main committee without amendment. We had a tremendous press for it. It was described as being more like the report of a royal commission, and when the debate took place in the House,

---

[18] Sir Richard Valentine Nind Hopkins (1880–1955), civil servant and key adviser to the treasury on financial policy and government expenditure 1927–45, permanent secretary of the Treasury 1942–5.

[19] Sir Horace John Wilson (1882–1972), civil servant, treasury adviser to Stanley Baldwin and Neville Chamberlain 1935–9, permanent secretary of the Treasury and head of the civil service 1939–42.

[20] William Strang, first Baron Strang (1893–1978), diplomat.

[21] George Tomlinson (1890–1952), politician, Labour MP for Farnworth 1938–1952, parliamentary secretary at the Ministry of Labour and National Service 1941–5, Minister of Works 1945–7, Minister of Education 1947–51.

the chairman of the whole committee – Sir John Wardlaw-Milne[22] – very generously only formally moved it and allowed me to explain the issues. This was possibly one of my best speeches in Parliament. Mr Pitman,[23] who was at the Treasury and later became a colleague in the House of Commons, told me that this report is used as the organisation and methods bible in the Treasury.

Towards the end of the war my committee investigated the question of disposals of war time surpluses and what preparations were being made to avoid the scandals that had occurred after the First World War. This experience became very valuable later on when, as a member of the government, I was placed in charge of the whole government machine to coordinate policy and ensure efficiency in disposals. This was purely accidental for I doubt if the Prime Minister had any knowledge of my select committee experience in this regard. Throughout life I have been in a way lucky – or one might interpret it as fate – in that chance has so often prepared me for some undertaking. While preparing lectures I have frequently just hit upon the very book I needed. My experience on the select committee in dealing with the Ministry of Supply made me *persona grata* when I went there as a minister, for they remembered my friendly help in their gruelling cross-examinations by the select committee where Herbert Williams nearly always heckled them as if they were in the dock.

I still acted – unpaid – as Scottish Secretary of the Labour Party for many months while the new appointment was being made, and I also took more than a full part in the work of the party in the House. It took more than the usual time in my case to damp the enthusiasm by which a new member comes in to put things right. There is a great weight of tradition in Parliament and in these days, seniority was of importance. MPs are difficult people to speak to and I found it very difficult in our party meetings to adopt the courtesies by which our southern colleagues as it were deferentially put their arguments. The result was that I was sometimes more blunt and thought to be talking to them like a teacher – as Tom Johnston warned me. But I found when I did attempt to adopt their more indirect style it was thought to be sarcasm, so I gave it up and said what I thought in my own way.

In these days Emmanuel Shinwell, Nye Bevan and some others were always 'agin the government'. Nye Bevan like Cripps was outside

---

[22] John Wardlaw-Milne (1879–1967), politician, Conservative MP for Kidderminster 1922–45.

[23] Isaac James Pitman (1901–45), businessman, educationist and politician, Conservative MP for Bath 1945–64, Director of Organisation and Methods at the Treasury 1943–5.

the party when I went to Parliament. But one day, Ness Edwards[24] came to me and sought my help. They were having a difficult miners' conference in Wales and they wanted Nye Bevan to be present to deal with the communists. It would be better, he said, if he were in the party and could I help? So I went and saw Greenwood and Attlee and they decided at a parliamentary party meeting to readmit him. The National Executive were very angry about it but it was done. His temperament made him an uneasy bedfellow. I used to describe some of our colleagues with this volatile temperament as the bucking broncos of the team. It was really difficult for them to keep within the races. Most of our people do not want fights and though I felt like that too I used to rise and oppose them when I thought they were driving us to a wrong conclusion. Adam McKinlay[25] used to become worried for me and wanted me to let someone else take the blows.

One day I nearly created a riot. The government were proposing to introduce supplementary allowances for miners' dependents depending on a family means test. Joe Batey,[26] one of the respected miners' MPs, wanted us to protest. A means test made the miners see red. I expressed the view that rather than just protest, we had better go forward with some policy we were willing to agree to, and that I did not think our Party, even in power, would abolish all forms of test. I raised a terrible storm about my ears but I stuck to my guns and when quiet was restored, I suggested we should have a committee of trades unionists who had experience of their own rules governing benefits, a local authority member with experience of public assistance, and a financial authority to work out whether we could have an individual income test. At the end, this was agreed to on Mr Attlee's motion and in the end, the committee came back with the recommendation that we go forward with the proposal for a personal income test just as we have for income tax. The government accepted the idea. The Determination of Needs Act was passed and removed for ever the humiliating family inquisition known as the 'means test'. Herbert Morrison[27] had not been there but

---

[24] Onesimus Edwards (1897–1968), trade unionist and politician, Labour MP for Caerphilly 1939–68, parliamentary secretary to the Minister of Labour and National Service 1945–50, postmaster-general 1950–1.

[25] Adam McKinlay (1887–1950), politician, Labour MP for Glasgow Partick 1929–31, Dunbartonshire 1941–50, Dunbartonshire West 1950.

[26] Joseph Batey (1867–1949), politician, Labour MP for Spennymoor 1922–42.

[27] Herbert Stanley Morrison, Baron Morrison of Lambeth (1888–1965), politician, MP for Hackney South 1923–4, 1929–31, 1935–45, Lewisham East 1945–50, Lewisham South 1950–9, Minister of Transport 1929–31, Minister of Supply 1940, Home Secretary 1940–5, Deputy Prime Minister 1945–51, Lord President of the Council 1945–51, Foreign Secretary 1951.

he told me afterwards he agreed with me and thought I had courage in daring to propose it.

Curiously enough, in 1943, in spite of my failure always to be pleasing, I was elected to the front bench. I regarded this as a very great honour, especially in view of my individual approach to problems. In 1940 the Chamberlain government collapsed and Mr Churchill formed a new national government with Mr Attlee as Deputy Prime Minister. Ernest Brown was Secretary of State for Scotland and when in 1941 Mr Churchill wanted Tom Johnston to become Minister of Health for England and Wales, Tom suggested it would be more suitable if Ernest Brown went there. So Tom became Secretary of State for Scotland and he invited me to become his Parliamentary Private Secretary. This is a purely private and unpaid appointment. A PPS is not a member of the government. He can exercise authority only insofar as he is acting for the Secretary of State.

The Scottish Office had not been accustomed to PPSs being very active but the Secretary of State and I were very close friends and he was very generous in giving me work to do and I was anxious to be as active as possible. I had a room both in London and in St Andrews House and was able to act as an aide-de-camp in all kinds of ways. I often deputised for him, though in official functions the under-secretaries and the law officers were his ministerial deputies. Joe Westwood and I were also good friends and I was always careful to ensure that my close connection with the Secretary of State never encroached on his province.

One useful thing I did was to visit the Polmont Institution. There I found these lads were shut up in cells at five o' clock and generally treated with the discipline of a normal prison. But they were being sent there not to be punished but reformed. I made a detailed report and suggested a number of changes – that the place should be brightened by repainting or distempered, that the boys should be treated as human beings and not as animals that had to be caged, that they should have physical and mental recreation in the evenings and generally be given the training they were sent there for to make them decent citizens. I even suggested well behaved lads getting home on parole as an encouragement. I am glad to say that all these ideas were adopted and they have worked very well. Now the boys at least get a chance. The trouble is that many of them are sub-normal but considerable success has been achieved with those that could be reclaimed.

I was a guest about twenty years later at the conference of prison officers when it was held in Scotland and the civil servant head of the department in the Scottish Office told me that he had been given the responsibility to carry out all the reforms of my original report to the

Secretary of State, and that these had caused a revolutionary change in the attitude to the use of borstal and other confinement from punishment to education and reform. I was surprised and Sir Charles Cunningham,[28] who became head of the Home Office, confirmed that my memo had started up a movement through all the penal systems of Britain. The Scots civil servant said he had spent the rest of his official life carrying the reforms into reality.

The wartime coalition was an innovation and there were many departures from normal procedure. In ordinary times, becoming a PPS was to take vows of silence so far as the ordinary work of the House was concerned. I broke away from several precedents. I declined to resign from the Select Committee on National Expenditure and while I observed loyal restraint in my minister's realm, I took a constructive part in the debates outside those of my minister's departments and responsibilities. I therefore sat, according to the debate, on either side of the House. When important speeches were being made, I used this privilege to sit facing the speaker as one could then get the full benefit of seeing and hearing.

I recall Lloyd George's last great speech on the occasion of the challenge to Chamberlain's government. He wound up with a biting peroration and all the more so in that it was delivered by a silver tongue and the culmination of a great build up. After complimenting Mr Chamberlain on his love of country, he said that it lay within the power of Mr Chamberlain tonight to do more for his country than any other man, and he then delivered the coup-de-grace – 'let him hand in his keys of Office'. Mr Amery[29] in that debate also turned thumbs down on his leader and implored him finally, 'For God's sake, Go!' On this occasion Mr Churchill wound up for the government defending Mr Chamberlain, little conscious that by the next day he would be Prime Minister. One of these unexpected scenes blew up in the middle of his speech. Mr Shinwell had interrupted him from the small gallery at the end of the House and Mr Churchill, who was never very fond of him, retorted something about 'skulking in the corner'. The Labour benches exploded. Neil McLean was protesting about the slur on Mr Shinwell. I was directly opposite Mr Churchill and said quietly to him – 'Why not withdraw?' He then banged his two firsts repeatedly on the dispatch box and shouted over and over again 'I won't withdraw – I won't withdraw'.

---

[28] Charles Cunningham (1906–98), civil servant, Scottish Home Department 1939–57, permanent Under-secretary of State at the Home Office 1957–66.
[29] Leopold Charles Maurice Stennett Amery (1873–1955), politician and journalist, MP for Birmingham South 1911–18, Birmingham Sparkbrook 1918–45, Secretary of State for the Colonies 1924–9 and for India 1940–5.

On other occasions when as Prime Minister he was speaking I returned to the Labour benches, for here it was possible to watch the changes of mood in Churchill's face which were almost as illuminating as his words. In one speech there would be clouds, sunshine, laughter and tears all following close on one another and on occasions when he was having a sly dig at America he would turn up the corner of his eyes to see the effect he was registering on Mr Kennedy,[30] the then United States ambassador.

On the occasion of the last and twilight speech of Lloyd George I was sitting in the PPS seat behind Mr Churchill and Mr Eden. Lloyd George was describing the sad plight of the nation. At the time there was a minor plot to shake the government and force them to invite Lloyd George to join them. In the midst of his jeremiad, Lloyd George got Iran and Iraq mixed up and referred to our treaty with one of them. Mr Eden and Churchill hurriedly consulted, asking each other if it was not the other way round, and I was asked – as is the duty of PPSs – to verify the position from the experts. They confirmed that Lloyd George was mistaken and Winston said 'we've got him' and when he came to reply, of course, he ridiculed very politely Lloyd George's confusion. Some days before this when I had mentioned to Hugh Dalton that there was a plot to get Lloyd George into the government, he said 'what use would that old Marshall Petain be?' This was reproduced in Churchill's speech when he said Lloyd George's defeatism reminded him of Marshall Petain. Lloyd George had a marvellously clear voice and could build up a powerful argument. He never raised his tones but spoke with piercing clarity. Lady Megan[31] had some of these qualities in her speeches and the qualities of the stable are more easily discernible in her than in Gwilym[32] – who was to become a member.

My experience in industry and my work on the select committee made it possible for me to contribute, I think, usefully in some of the debates on the war, especially where they concerned production problems. In one debate on production and manpower I referred to the need for settling priorities within the government itself. I understand that when Herbert Morrison reported to the Cabinet that as Minister of Supply, he had been able to get some valuable machinery out of France

[30] Joseph Patrick Kennedy (1888–1969), American businessman and politician, US Ambassador to the court of St James 1938–40.

[31] Megan Arfon Lloyd George (1902–66), politician, Liberal MP for Anglesey 1929–51, Labour MP for Carmarthen 1957–66.

[32] Gwilym Lloyd George, first Viscount Tenby (1894–1967), politician, National Liberal MP for Pembrokeshire 1922–3, Liberal MP for Pembrokeshire, 1923–4, 1929–50, National Liberal Conservative MP for Newcastle upon Tyne North 1951–7, Minister for Fuel and Power 1942–5, Minister of Food 1951–4, Minister for Welsh Affairs and Home Secretary 1954–7.

and that it was being brought to Southampton, Lord Beaverbrook, as Minister of Aircraft, shanghaied it on behalf of his Ministry. I said:

> A very lovable old sea raider had been placed in charge of the Ministry of Aircraft Production. Nobody doubts his capacity as a scoop reporter or a man who can get what he wants, but the man to put in charge of a sea raider against the enemy is the last man to place in charge of a cruiser that is part of the battle fleet, because a different temperament is wanted.

I mention this because it brought from Mr Churchill, who followed me, one of his famous epigrams. After referring to my description of Lord Beaverbrook as 'an old sea raider', he said that was 'a euphemistic method of describing a pirate' [and] he added, 'he is a man of altogether exceptional force and genius who is at his very best when things are at their very worst'. I cannot say I was one of Churchill's intimates but on occasions, he sat down beside me in the smoke room and talked about different matters. At the time of the first secret session he explained why thought the secret session was right. He felt that Members of Parliament were very special people and in a war, when necessarily their liberty of free speech was curtailed, it was necessary to make clear to the public that MPs were the safeguard of liberty, that the House of Commons was the most important body in the land and that in the long run, he was its servant. Nothing really vital could, of course, be disclosed but there was more freedom of discussion. One MP was charged with a breach of privilege for having discussed matters from the secret session and that certainly enhanced the mystery. The Prime Minister later published his secret session speeches in book form. All his speeches during this period were carefully prepared not only for the benefit of the House, but he was very conscious that he was making history and he was deliberately writing it at the same time.

On another occasion, when I was one of a small group of ministers and ex-ministers waiting for a royal audience, Mr Churchill came over and gave me his views on the Scots. He thought they were a great race and had made a valuable contribution to our society in every walk of life. Mr Attlee, wondering no doubt what he was talking about, joined us and I was glad, for I was not sure that he took the same view of Scots. Mr Attlee did admire the Clyde group in the earlier days for their fight in the House but Mr Churchill had had a wider and closer acquaintanceship with Scots in Scotland and in politics. Herbert Morrison used to say he could never quite understand the Scots and Mr Attlee had, I believe, the same difficulty.

About 1943 I was asked to go on a parliamentary delegation to New Zealand. At the same time, unfortunately Mr Greenwood came to me with the request that I should become a member of the Speaker's Conference on Parliamentary Reform. He pointed out that with my experience of electioneering in Scotland it was desirable that I should represent the Scots. So I had to forego the journey to NZ and I spent some months on the Speaker's Conference. Scotland's representation in the House of Commons was threatened by the increase of relative population in England. With my Irish and Welsh colleagues, we were able to keep our representation intact.

When the House discussed the implementation of the report, I had words with Herbert Morrison who was inclined to think Scotland was 'getting away with it again', and when he referred sentimentally to the retention of the City of London, I asked him to realise that mathematical calculation could not determine Scotland's share if sentiment was to be considered in London. When the report came before the House, I was given the honour of stating on behalf of the party its position on the question of proportional representation. I tried to make it one of the fullest expositions of the pros and cons of this complex question. My election experience involved me also at the end of the war in service on an inter-party committee under Sir John Anderson on arrangements for the post-war election, especially how the services were to be able to vote.

The end of the war brought the break-up of the coalition and our leaders returned to their own benches. After my election to the front bench in 1943, I ceased to decide the subjects of my speeches which were, of course, thenceforward on behalf of the party. It is a sacrifice one must make of the right to be a freelance and have a choice of intervention at any time, on acceptance of nomination for what I regard as the greater one of being a spokesman for the party. My main job from then on was, however, my favourite subjects of industry and finance. Our principal leaders being in the government, Pethick Lawrence[33] spoke as number one on budget matters but usually I was number two or three as the case arose. I spoke therefore on many budgets and other financial questions. On the break-up of the coalition, the ex-ministers, of course, took on much of the front bench work and our opportunities for speaking were spread out more thinly.

In these days also we had much friction and many attempts were made to apply discipline. Even our front bench used to divide

---

[33] Frederick William Pethick-Lawrence, Baron Pethick-Lawrence (1871–1961), politician, Labour MP for Leicester West 1923–31, Edinburgh East 1935–45, Financial Secretary to the Treasury 1929–31.

sometimes into opposite lobbies. There were continual plots to overthrow the Churchill government and the House was occasionally divided crosswise. Curious coalitions developed for this purpose. At one time, Sir John Wardlaw-Milne, the chairman of the powerful Select Committee on National Expenditure, was associated with Nye Bevan and others on both sides in a powerful vote of censure on the government. The attack which was mounted was really formidable and the House was packed. The whole attack, however, collapsed because of an interpolation into Wardlaw Milne's speech. No one knows to this day whether it was just a mental aberration or whether it was deliberate. He was pointing out the need for a supreme commander who could eliminate the inter-service conflicts and then suddenly he stopped and suggested a name – the duke of Gloucester.[34] The House roared and then melted away. A reputation and a rebellion were punctured by the same slip.

Another unexpected partnership which developed then was that between Earl Winterton[35] and Emanuel Shinwell. The House has a genius for coining appropriate nicknames and this partnership provoked one of the most apt of all. There was a play running at the Adelphi which provided the combination's name – 'Arsenic and Old Lace'. James Walker,[36] that powerful and logical Scot, once said about Shinwell that he had great ability but all his life had suffered from an irreconcilable contradiction – that he wanted to be a rebel and a statesman at the same time. This describes him completely. This internal conflict kept him out of the government during the war. He had been offered the parliamentary secretaryship to the Ministry of Food under Lord Woolton[37] and refused. He says he disliked coalitions but the general view was that having been a minister – of Mines – in a previous government, he refused to be demoted. Another consideration I believe might have influenced him. Though he made a good and efficient minister, he loves the battle and he must have recognised that there would be a nominal 'leader of the opposition' and some say he expected that he would be elected. In the event,

---

[34] Prince Henry, first duke of Gloucester (1900–74), third son of George V.
[35] Edward Turnour, sixth Earl Winterton (1883–1962), politician, Conservative MP for Horsham 1904–51, Chancellor of the Duchy of Lancaster 1937–9, father of the House of Commons 1945–51.
[36] James Walker (1883–1945), trade unionist and politician, ILP member and Glasgow City councillor 1912–29, Labour MP for Newport 1929–31, Motherwell 1935–45.
[37] Frederick James Marquis, first early of Woolton (1883–1964), politician and businessman, Minister of Food 1940–3, Minister of Reconstruction 1943–5, Chairman of the Conservative Party 1946–55.

Lees Smith[38] was elected and Mannie fell between two stools. His knowledge of shipping was put to good use and he also specialised for a time on empire questions with Lord Winterton. He did a tremendous lot of work both in and out of the House. He was tireless in carrying out engagements in the country and must have had few weekends at home. As he says in his book, he, like Churchill, knows what it is to be alone and that in some ways has been his life. He was never a team man in the sense that he subordinated the rebel for the statesman.

At my first Labour Party Conference at Birmingham, I recall his devastating ridicule of the illogicalities of the ILP of which he was a leader, but noticing the obvious pleasure this was giving the platform, he then proceeded to rend them. He was an excellent debater and made his mark from his first speech but he tended to be too confident at the dispatch box which, curiously enough, irritates the House. Nothing keeps him down which also is displeasing to many MPs who do not like any of their number hogging the limelight. But that never bothers Mannie. He has always decided his own line without fear or favour. He gets great fun out of the fight. His guiding philosophy was well described in the title of his book *Conflict without Malice.*[39]

Fame or notoriety is an essential element of political distinction. The most difficult way to get this is by hard work and good sense, which gather no headlines. The able politician who has a policy must therefore flood-light it by dramatic presentation or even sensational colouring. Churchill was the greatest artist of them all in dramatising his politics. He staged all his appearances as historical events. Mr Attlee was the exact opposite. It was impossible to get him to illuminate his leadership with any kind of spectacular accompaniment. Only a freak of chance could have made him leader of our Party since he had neither ambition nor personal push and his is one of the cases – as is that also of Churchill to some extent – where conditions determined the leadership rather than any success in a contest.

Many people during the war attained world publicity because they attacked Mr Churchill. To be associated with him even in that form attracted notice. I had a curious experience myself of this. When Hess[40] landed in Scotland everyone tried to guess the reason. I have always had a great respect for the wiles of our secret service. The admiral who founded our modern naval intelligence services wrote a very interesting history. He indicated the principles on which countries acted. The Germans, he said, made war on the principles of intimidate

---

[38] Hastings Bertrand Lees-Smith (1878–1941), politician, MP for Northampton 1910–18, Keighley 1922–3, 1924–31, 1935–41, Leader of the Opposition 1940–1.
[39] Emanuel Shinwell, *Conflict without Malice: An Autobiography* (London, 1955).
[40] Rudolf Walter Richard Hess (1894–1987), Deputy Führer to Adolf Hitler 1933–41.

and terrify, while the British worked on the principle of mislead and mystify. I suspected that they had mystified and misled Rudolf Hess or Hitler. At the time, some Scottish nationalists had been imprisoned for collecting bombs and it seemed possible that Hess had been persuaded that Scotland was ready to contract out of the war. I therefore put down a question to Churchill asking him whether there was any truth in the theory that our intelligence people had misled Hess in this fashion and induced him to come to Scotland. He replied characteristically that that was one mistake Hitler could not make – to think that Scotland would give in.

Which recalls one of the best stories of the war. Two Scots soldiers were standing on the quay at Dover after the retreat from Dunkirk. One looked rather glum and his friend said, 'What's the matter, Jock. Are you down hearted?' The other sadly replied, 'Aye. I'm worried. If the English give in, this is going to be a long war'.

When the war ended and our part of the government front bench came over to our own side, it was interesting that the only person who refused – as he did till he retired – to say one bitter personal word to or about Churchill was Clement Attlee. In the debates which took place between them there was always the greatest personal respect for each other. As we were all walking out of the chamber, I actually heard Churchill congratulate Attlee on a speech in a major debate during which he punctured successfully every argument Churchill had put forward. This indeed was the result of every debate they had with each other starting with their controversy over Laski.[41] Winston loved graphic phrases and never hesitated to sacrifice accuracy for dramatic effect. Clem Attlee, on the other hand, analysed every argument with the relentless logic of the comptometer – one point making another – till Churchill's colourful rhetorical butterflies were reduced to their rather meagre skeletons. The curious thing is that each respected the qualities which the other had and which he himself lacked. Seldom have there been two more widely different personalities so effectively complementary.

In the wartime Cabinet I believe this is how progress was made. Winston supplied the inspiration and drive and Clem translated it into practical terms. It is, of course, history now as to how Mr Churchill misjudged the electorate after the war and shocked them by his somersault from praising his erstwhile colleagues as great comrades

---

[41]   Harold Joseph Laski (1893–1950), political theorist, Professor of Political Science, London School of Economics 1926–50. Churchill named Laski in a radio broadcast in June 1945 as the man who would control a Labour government through the National Executive Committee.

in the struggle to describing them as masters of ogres and Gestapos threatening the liberties of the people.

It was a curious thing to see Winston in opposition. He reminded me of Donna Anna in hell, the scene in Bernard Shaw's *Man and Superman* where she asks to see the devil to find out why she should be there and to have the mistake rectified. Winston never understood how the electors had suddenly brought him down from world leader to chief critic on the opposition front bench and he was never satisfied till he could, like Donna Anna, have the mistake rectified. As Clem Attlee used to tell him, having played a match and lost, he wanted to play it over again. On one of the many occasions when he was making speech on the terrible sufferings and disasters brought about by the Labour government and how we were all ruined, someone interjected 'Sell your horse', which brought the House down. He retorted immediately 'Well I could do that and no doubt benefit but having listened to the socialists, I eschew the profit motive.'

CHAPTER EIGHT

The election over and Labour returned with a huge majority, there was the question of forming a government. Theoretically and in practice, Labour elected its leader annually and a change was possible at any time. In 1922 when there was a great influx of Labour MPs including the Clyde group, Mr Clynes was displaced and Ramsay MacDonald was elected leader in his place. There were some suggestions, attributed to Herbert Morrison, that this great new Parliament should start from scratch and choose its Prime Minister. The constitutional practice when a government loses an election is for the Prime Minister to resign and recommend the Crown to send for the Leader of the Opposition and invite him to form a government. Ernest Bevin was against a new election and, it is believed, advised Clem Attlee who had already had the invitation of the King to go ahead and form his Government. In any case, at a meeting we held of the new MPs, the other idea evaporated and was never voiced since there was no inclination to change the leadership.

I was later informed that at first I was chosen to go to the Treasury as Financial Secretary but in the final placing some others were less easily placed and that it was easier to shift me round. I was eventually sent to Aircraft Production. When this was proposed, I was not very enthusiastic about the idea and I rather think it arose from the fact that Clem had been in the chamber when I had to deliver a speech on civil aviation which rather impressed him.

It was curious how this arose. I was a relatively new and junior boy on the front bench and naturally, in selecting the party spokesman in major debates, all the leading speeches were allocated to the senior leaders and ex-ministers. On this occasion, about two days before the debate, Fred Montague,[1] who had been a minister in this department, called off and was unable to take the debate. I rather fancy that none of

---

[1] Frederick Montague (1876–1966), politician, Labour MP for Islington West 1923–31, 1935–47.

the others felt like risking plunging into this new subject at such short notice but in any case, I was appointed to lead the debate. I had some background engineering savvy and I spent a hard two days on the job. In the debate, I held my own in the face of the usual interruptions which soon discover weaknesses in anyone who does not know his case. Unless one has steeped himself in a subject he is always liable to be caught out by one of the many experts who is certain to be lying in wait for a slip.

However, I accepted Mr Attlee's appointment and went to my office which had used to be Sir Alfred Mond's room in Millbank. John Wilmot[2] was at the Ministry of Supply offices in the Strand and was to carry on the two offices till they were eventually merged as Minister of Supply and Aircraft Production. I found him a good minister to work under. His job at the Ministry of Supply was so big that he was quite pleased to leave me to look after the aircraft production side, though it took a little time to get the civil service to accept the parliamentary secretary as having any authority. They eventually found that with the minister's many preoccupations, by coming to me they could get things done. I had learned while on the select committee that a parliamentary secretary had really no duties constitutionally and in the organisation of the Ministry of Supply, they had tried to allocate him some responsibility. I realised that any junior minister can only act vicariously for his minister and John Wilmot was quite pleased to leave me to look after aircraft and was generous in devolving quite a lot of authority on me.

As I gained the confidence of the staff I was able to map out my own activities and initiate policy in many cases. I took part in the various committees of heads of departments. One at that time was the design and production of the aluminium house. This was a scientifically designed house to utilise the capacity of the aircraft works which were becoming redundant and to utilise the scrap aluminium which would result from the break-up of aircraft. It was like a major military operation. The possibility of their transport by road, the design of special carriers, and a multitude of ancillary problems had to be solved in addition to the production of the house. As designed, it was nearly a perfect little house. But when huge numbers began to come off the lines, we ran into shortages of various materials and substitutes had to be found or modifications of the design were made and these, of

---

[2]   John Wilmot, 1st Baron Wilmot of Selmeston (1893–1964), politician, Labour MP for Fulham East 1933–5, Lambeth Kennington 1939–45, Deptford 1945–50, Minister of Supply 1945–7.

course, brought troubles of condensation and other defects which detracted from the original.

It used often to be said why not produce houses as we would tanks? We eventually were producing these houses quicker than any tanks had been produced and in far greater numbers. At one time, a house was coming off the assembly line every ten minutes. At Dumbarton one forenoon, I signed my name on four parts of a complete house as it left the factory and at four in the afternoon – about five hours later – I and the press were having tea in the house outside Paisley on the other side of the Clyde, erected, with water and electricity turned on. They nicknamed them in Tillicoultry 'Woodburn's wee wonders'.

I became involved almost immediately in terrific problems about aircraft. Ernest Bevin, Foreign Secretary, was having difficulty in international negotiations because there was a tendency for both America and Russia to treat Britain as if it didn't matter. It was important therefore 'to show the flag' and one of the ways was to have British aircraft opening up civil aviation all over the world.

It might be wondered at how Britain was being pushed into the background. Both Stalin and Roosevelt had felt they were the two great arbiters of the world's destiny. They looked on Britain as a discredited imperialist whose empire was due for the scrap yard. They went behind Churchill's back and fixed up all kinds of deals on their own. It was as a result of these deals that Russia was able to occupy Berlin and be in a position to take over Poland and other parts of eastern Europe.

To re-establish Britain's prestige required civilian aircraft. But it had been a condition of America's policy of sending us munitions and goods under the policy they called 'Lease Lend' that this would not be used for Britain's own development and that all our efforts would be directed to winning the war. This meant that Britain for six years could do nothing towards the design and production of civil aircraft. America with its huge resources had been able to go ahead with her progress in this field. It took about six years to reach the point where a new design actually got into service so that starting in 1945 we could not hope for new aircraft till about 1951. We had, as the only possibility, to adapt war time machines for civil purposes. Lancasters, Yorks and Sunderland flying boats were all converted. We could not be prevented from planning for peace.

A committee under Lord Brabazon[3] had meantime produced a scheme for the design and production of every kind of civilian aircraft.

[3] John Theodore Cuthbert Moore-Brabazon (1884–1964), politician and aviator, Conservative MP for Rochester Chatham 1918–29, Wallasey 1931–42, Minister of Transport 1940–1, Minister of Aircraft Production 1941–2.

Firms were selected to specialise on aircraft for the various needs and they got down to the job. Bristol aircraft were made responsible for the London-New York non-stop; De Haviland for the express type; two firms were to design a commonwealth world type, and two firms were to produce a domestic and European type. There was to be a smaller plane to feed the larger planes from minor airfields.

I had the greatest trouble with the Ministry of Civil Aviation. Their people seem to be sold on American aircraft and it fell to me sometimes almost to compel them to order British. The Ambassador – later called the Elizabethan – was considered by our experts to be a great aircraft but the Civil Aviation Ministry were most reluctant to order it. What happened was that, with the exception of the Brabazon type which was too big to duplicate and was given to the Bristol Company to develop, in all other cases more than one egg was being hatched out and in the range of the Ambassador and the Viscount, both were first class aircraft. The four-engined Viscount was preferred to the Ambassador whose two engines were no longer acceptable for oversea passenger flights. The same happened with the Dove which was to be the 'feeder' plane. It is expensive for an airline to have too many models and it naturally wants the best.

I was daily being asked by other ministers about delays in delivering the planes and this alone would have required me to make myself informed on the whole problem and I confess I found the exercise both interesting and instructive. Discussions with those responsible for research and production kept me in touch with all that was happening and going to happen and with the intense public interest. As the minister actively responsible, I had to give periodic press conferences about our progress. It has been a satisfying experience to see these conceptions announced ten to twenty years before taking the air and capturing the world's imagination. That did not help me much in the face of the pressure of 1948.

Occasionally, in these days deputising for the minister I had to attend at meetings of the Cabinet and the Lord President's Committee presided over by Herbert Morrison. The purpose of this committee was to coordinate the work of ministers responsible for economic and social policy. Herbert Morrison at this time had assumed responsibility for the general economic planning of the government and, though responsible himself for no department, tried to keep in touch with the work of all the ministers. In addition, he was the Leader of the House and a prominent member of the National Executive and its policy-forming committees.

Herbert was a tremendous worker and was credited with ambition. Whether it was justified or not, he was always suspected of scheming and Ernest Bevin and others seemed to think it their duty to thwart him. When he introduced the London Passenger Transport Scheme, he stood up to the Transport and General Workers Union in some of their demands and at the annual conference faced a violent attack on his policy. In such matters he had both courage and obstinacy. He was always a fighter. On occasions when others were more timid to stand up to the communists in their infiltration into the movement, Herbert got the job of dealing with them. His only peer in this matter was James Walker of the Iron and Steel Trades Federation. His arguments had irresistible logic and he spoke with all the force of the steam hammers associated with his trade. For years Herbert and myself were the main antagonists of the Communist Party. Herbert was a tower of strength in keeping the Labour Party steady while I had weekly articles during the whole period in the *Forward* refuting Communist Party theory and practice, not mere abuse of the CP but showing the impracticability of their policy on the basis of their own philosophy. The quotations I used provided our people throughout the country with sound replies to the seemingly well informed arguments of the Communist Party.

Ever since Chartist times there have always been diverse approaches to the problems of power and prior to the war, arguments were less about what would or could be done by a Labour government but whether a Labour government could get power at all, and whether if it became the government and tried to introduce its policy there would not be effective sabotage by the capitalists. The communists concluded that the only eventual way would be by armed revolution. I have always been fond of parables to bring points home and one of the miners' leaders – Joe Waugh – provided me with a useful story to debunk the illusion of salvation by the destruction of capitalism. A young communist miner went to work in a gas-threatened pit. When the men gathered for their mid-day snack, the older miners were horrified to see the newcomer take out a pipe and matches. They immediately pounced on him saying 'you cannot do that here – you'll blow up the pit', to which he replied 'What the hell does that matter, it is the capitalist's pit anyway!' As with Low's cartoons the point got home without long discussion. The communists used to send people to meetings to heckle speakers in order to get publicity for their policies but they stopped attending my meetings, I was told, because it provided the opportunity and invited the refutation of their arguments.

Herbert Morrison did a great job nationally in this respect and once said to me that he sometimes felt that the brunt of the battle was left to him and me. Probably due to Scots being steeped in polemics as a result of generations of church disputes, I rather enjoyed the arguments and I must say the communists appreciated that I did not use abuse but argued the case. This type of argument has largely disappeared. The coming of the Labour government in 1945 made the power argument appear theoretical polemics. Victory in 1945 brought us up against the practical problems. Herbert's feeling that he had an overall responsibility and his insistence on keeping so many strings in his own hands brought about a breakdown which took the form of a thrombosis which laid him low for some months. It was a striking indication of how little even the greatest of us count that his absence caused no disturbance of the political water which flowed on as before. Stafford Cripps stepped into the shoes of Herbert as the controller of our economic planning.

When Herbert returned to the Cabinet he for a time had to listen to Cripps till Attlee found it useful to restore his precedence by inviting his observations on all important matters. Though I was still a junior minister, I was, however, given responsibility for coordinating all the work of disposals of surplus war stores which, of course, was a major operation and full of pitfalls. I recall a deputation from workers in the wireless valve industry protesting that the cutting down of their work was going to cause unemployment and at the same time objecting to the destruction of thousands of surplus valves. I had to point out that the two demands were mutually destructive. In our plans, we had to maintain and help a valve-producing industry. If we put all the valves left over from the war on the market they would supply the country's needs for about ten years by which time their industry would be dead. So, of the two alternatives, we had to preserve their industry. Because of considerations such as this, all disposals were released on to the market only in such a way as not to prevent the recovery of industry.

We had a mass of material out in Egypt. With the demand for speedy demobilisation, we were steadily losing the men necessary to guard these millions of pounds' worth of stores. At best of times it was difficult to protect them. About this time, the groundnut scheme was developing and it needed crawler tractors to pull down trees and clear the ground and for operations in the building of the docks. We had no way of cataloguing what was in these dumps nor were we urgently concerned to deal with them until we could move them, so we sold them to the groundnut scheme which had the job of searching for what it needed among all available material. The government got the money for the surpluses so that at least much of the so-called loss by the groundnuts scheme was already added to the money gained by the surplus sales.

At this time, the need for crawler tractors was a major concern of the government and actually a committee of the highest level had to be appointed to allocate any that came to light. Open cast mining needed them, the groundnuts scheme needed them and some of our vital purchases from abroad were dependent on our supplying these in exchange for vital imports from other countries. It is hard to believe that on two occasions, the most vital exports our government had to find were hoes for Siam when rice was the key to peace in the east and crawler tractors which were a universally acceptable currency. At that time world exports prophesied a world famine in fats in five years. There was no time to have long debates – action had to be taken. The most expert firm in this country advised a great drive to cultivate groundnuts to save the situation, and after experts had examined their proposition, they were authorised to proceed. The firm found it too much for them so on their advice, a government company was formed which ran into the snags of two unexpected dry years and other technical problems which ruined all expectations. But at the time, the scheme was welcomed by Oliver Stanley on behalf of the Tories and there has been no more dishonest political stunt than the wise-after-the-event campaign of the Tories on the failure of the groundnuts scheme.

On the research side, I was responsible for our captures of equipment on the continent as well, and my first journey there was in connection with our taking over the German research stations in Volkenrode and Göttingen. Volkenrode was in the midst of a forest, and the Germans had actually trees growing on the roofs of the buildings so that nothing could be seen from the sky. There we found what was one of the finest wind tunnels in the world for testing aircraft speed problems. Curiously enough, the German scientists has never been allowed to see their own instrument at work for they were excluded when the aircraft firms came to test their secret models. The German scientists were very interested therefore to see with our scientists how perfectly their machine functioned. What was in appearance an old German farmhouse had a marvellous range for testing rifle fire. We collected the lot and brought some of the scientists over here to help us. They were unwilling to come unless they could bring their wives because they did not want them left to the starvation conditions in Germany. I could understand this but it would have been political dynamite to give new houses to Germans when our own people were in such desperate need. However, their knowledge was of key value so I got the problem solved by providing hostels. One of the greatest of them, a Dr Schmidt,[4] was killed in our service by an explosion a year or two

[4]   Johannes Schmidt (1903–47), rocket technician, designed and developed rocket motor for ME163 and died in an explosion during a test at the rocket propulsion

afterwards. The Russians were at this time making generous offers to tempt these men to Russia and a few had already gone.

I flew in every kind of aircraft. When I visited a factory as the minister, I was expected to experience the latest advance. I went up in an early helicopter; I flew at 20,000 feet in the first pressurised aircraft – another forgotten British achievement; I went up in the first civil plane to fly with jet propulsion; I landed in a Firefly on an aircraft carrier (after two attempts) and saw the first jet planes land on deck. I remember the first apparatus to test out the pilot ejector apparatus, which later saved many lives, and I handled the first models of a future engineless aeroplane of which we are seeing the beginnings in the artificial satellites.

My companions through Germany were a representative of the Treasury and Air Marshall Alex [sic] Coryton[5] who was Chief Executive of Research and Development. Out visit took in Volkenrode, Göttingen, Hanover and Berlin. Berlin in 1946 was a tragic sight. The government buildings were still scattered over the ground and I was able to rummage among heaps of wet and sodden foreign office documents scattered among the ruins of the imperial German empire.

We visited Hitler's chancellery and were going to see the bunker, only to be held up by a Mongolian-type Russian soldier. Air Vice Marshall Davidson, commanding Berlin, advised us not to persist as these soldiers were not able to reason about their orders and would probably fire first. At that time, there was a curious scene outside the old Reichstag buildings. Hundreds of people from both the Russian and other sections gathered for one of the blackest markets in history. Jewellery of all kinds – probably loot – was exchanged for food, cigarettes, and necessities of all kind. Viewed from the road it was like a swarm of struggling ants.

During my service as under minister, I had few occasions for speaking in the House as the Ministry of Supply was not a department much in the field of political controversy, except in discussions on the aluminium house and disposals, for both of which issues I had special responsibility. I did speak in aircraft debates usually in partnership with Civil Aviation. I had, however, an unforgettable experience in this department which was an education from beginning to end which for me was a combination of work and pleasure.

department, Westcott, *Times*, 14 November 1947.

[5] William Alec Coryton (1895–1981), RAF officer, Controller of Research and Development in the Ministry of Aircraft Production 1945–50, Chief Executive for Guided Weapons at Ministry of Supply 1950–1.

CHAPTER NINE

I got a message one day in Edinburgh to phone the Prime Minister. I did so from St Andrews House on the private phone and was invited to become Secretary of State for Scotland. Joe Westwood had resigned. No greater honour could befall a Scot and though I was genuinely reluctant to leave the Ministry of Supply which had been so very much up my street, I went into the new office with at least the determination to do what I could for Scotland.

Joe Westwood was my immediate predecessor. He was a remarkable man. A miner, he had been truly educated in the school of experience with a great background of local government, parliamentary service and various royal and other commissions. He had a mind like a needle and could pick up things speedily. Even he would not have claimed to have the originality and fertility of ideas of Tom Johnston but he was a fighter. I do not know the conditions of his resignation but he went out of office with dignity, and during his remaining lifetime he was as loyal and friendly to me as he had been during our long association before and during the war.

I knew it was possible to build a reputation at the Scottish Office by pretending to be, as I described it, a Scottish St George fighting the English dragon in the shape of my colleagues in the Cabinet, but I made clear in my first speech to the Scottish Council of the Labour Party that I felt this attitude was to demean the importance of the Secretary of State being a member of the Cabinet. He was not there only to keep his colleagues informed on its progress, problems and needs, but to accept equal responsibility with his other colleagues for running the whole country. Scotland did not need to beg for favours so long as she had rights. There was no reason to doubt that these would be infringed in any way.

This was at a period when the Tories had linked their campaign with that of the Scottish nationalists and Joe Westwood had been under great pressure. The day I took office I came right up against this problem. The local authorities had wanted the fire brigades denationalised and handed back to local government. Arrangements had to be made for settling wages and conditions of service. The unions wanted national negotiations so that anomalies would not be created. The local authorities throughout Britain could not agree. Some wanted to negotiate direct as local authorities, some wanted to negotiate through the National Joint Council, and Scotland was further divided with one delegation asking for separate Scottish negotiations. I tried to get the purpose for this cleared up, for I would have supported it had there been any advantage. But I could get no reply to my queries. Was the purpose to pay higher wages in Scotland? Was it to pay lower wages? Was it to pay the same wages? If the last, were these rates to be negotiated in Scotland and followed by England, or negotiated in England and followed later by Scotland as was usually the case? If the same wages were to be paid, was it not necessary to have them settled jointly as the unions wanted? It was difficult to see Scottish local authorities wanting to pay higher rates and the unions in Scotland would not accept lower wages. Eventually there was no agreed policy among the Scottish local authorities and my recollection is that the Secretary of State had to use his powers to prescribe uniform rates.

These are the practical problems which surrounded the problems raised by Scottish nationalism. When Eric Geddes[1] had proposed after the first world war to establish an independent Scottish railway system as part of the reorganisation, the agitation by Scottish chambers of commerce, industrialists, and trades unions – especially the railwaymen – led to such an agitation in the House of Commons that the proposal had to be withdrawn. It was argued that Scottish railways could not live and pay decent wages as an independent unit. Miners, because of different and poor coal seams, had always had lower rates and in England and generally speaking, the workers found that they get better conditions as the result of national organisations. No government at that time could have dared suggest to the miners a return to district wage negotiations.

However, there was another side to the question. I do not believe over-centralisation to be a good thing and it is in my view essential for democracy that government should be as near and intimate to the people as possible. I did not think, however, that Scots people would be willing to make too big an economic sacrifice for the satisfaction of 'governing themselves', especially as I knew that Northern Ireland

[1]   Eric Campbell Geddes (1875–1937), politician and businessman, First Lord of the Admiralty 1917–19, Minister of Transport 1919–21, Conservative MP for Cambridge 1917–22.

did not want self-government and even now had grave doubts about its 'advantages'. Nor did I feel that any of us really wanted to reduce Scottish rights and influence in the British House of Commons, where our United Kingdom had established the greatest example of cooperation between nations in the history of the world.

I therefore proceeded at once to examine this problem with these conditions in mind to see how far we could devolve the responsibilities of government. I tackled first of all the constitutional position. Could Scottish parliamentary powers be increased without sacrificing existing rights? The Scottish Grand Committee was an obvious instrument. One proposal had been on the stocks for many years but no one seemed to have done anything about it – empowering the committee to discuss Scottish estimates – and I embodied this in my scheme. I added the right to debate the second reading of bills. The advantage of this is that when the House of Commons programme is choked up with work, non-controversial but quite important bills might be crushed out by the impossibility to find time for their second reading. I drafted my proposals and then gave them to the Scottish civil service experts for examination. They came to say that a proposal had been considered many years before but was found unworkable. I had not known this but fortunately, I was able to point out that my suggestions had avoided the snag which had wrecked the previous one. The experts at once agreed and the next step was to discuss it with the constitutional advisers to the House. I had a tough assignment to convert Sir Gilbert Campion,[2] the Principal Clerk of the House, but finally I succeeded.

Outside the House I thought that the real need for Scottish self-government was in industry and, as this was almost entirely in the hands of private enterprise, what was needed was some mechanism of coordinating and guiding our Scottish national development. This, it appeared to me, should be a council of representatives of all agencies which controlled the economic life of Scotland – the government, the representatives of British departments in Scotland, the nationalised industries, the British Council which embraced local authorities, industrialists, trades unions etc. These combined to create the Scottish Economic Conference. Every organisation which controlled the economic life of Scotland was represented directly or indirectly. Under the chairmanship of the Secretary of State, there was a two-way exchange of information and views and the Chancellor of the

---

[2] Gilbert Francis Montriou Campion, Baron Campion (1882–1958), civil servant, clerk to the House of Commons 1937–48 and expert on parliamentary procedure, with publications such as *Introduction to the Procedure of the House of Commons* (1929) and his edition (the fourteenth) of Sir Thomas Erskine May's *Parliamentary Practice* (1946).

Exchequer and other ministers came as guests to explain their policies and plans.

However, the whole plan had to be approved by Parliament. In preparation, I invited the Scottish leaders of the parties in the House to discuss the draft and give me their views. The Conservatives had some qualms about the proposals for having the second reading of bills in committee but they all agreed and I was then able to go to my colleagues for their endorsement. The new standing orders were drafted with the assistance of Sir Gilbert Campion, the Clerk to the House, and Parliament itself unanimously approved. It was interesting for me some years later when I was a member of a committee to consider how to deal with statutory instruments, that the Clerks to the House advised us to look at the success of the Scottish Grand Committee method of dealing with bills, though in the early stages I had a tough assignment gaining their approval. The system has worked. The Royal Commission which later considered these two matters did not see how further devolution was possible without virtually removing Scottish business from the floor of the House.

Objection had been made that on these second reading debates we do not vote in the committee. This is a misconception of what takes place in Parliament. Oppositions and MPs in general do not win their points by votes – no government would risk a defeat in that way. Most victories are gained by argument and debate, and Scottish MPs gained a great addition to their parliamentary opportunities to influence events.

The Scottish Economic Conference had a different fate. It was criticised because the press were not admitted. This was impracticable without condemning many of its members to silence for, of course, no civil servant nor chairman of a nationalised board could speak freely if his remarks were to be reported. The virtue of this economic parliament was to be its informality. In the period of my chairmanship, there was great need to keep everyone informed about policy and get an understanding cooperation. I agree that in periods where nothing new is being done or proposed there is less need, and this evidently was the view of my successors for it has never been called again to meet. Yet it was an outlet for Scottish opinion and its departure without complaint implies that it was superfluous and that therefore Scotland does not need more expression. Herbert Morrison was impressed by its work and used it as a model for his creation of a Welsh Council which has continued ever since.

These things have to grow in our country and had I continued to be responsible for Scottish affairs, it was my hope that we might have an annual economic conference on a wider scale in public which would have given expression to Scottish views on the economic field, much as the Convention of Royal Burghs debates local government affairs. Governments, of course, do not like bodies which are almost bound to be critical and I should think it likely the opportunity has now gone.

During the war, Tom Johnston brought together a council of ex-Secretaries of State which in the period of the war was a great success. It included three Cabinet ministers and in the days of coalition enabled Tom to prepare the ground for his proposals and start off with a measure of agreement. It was not practicable in the more controversial atmosphere of party politics. The opposition could not commit themselves through their representative and tie their tongues when the business came before Parliament. So it had to be dropped though it was a valuable council of state.

My next step towards devolution was to consult those who were responsible in Scotland for the nationalised industries to seek their view as to how far they needed greater powers in Scotland. They all said they had all the powers they needed and it seemed unwise to create any unnecessary barriers merely for the sake of being separate. I then set to work to deal with Scotland as a whole. From my own experience as an under-secretary I realised how important it was for the minister to bring his colleagues into the picture and therefore I invited all my fellow Scottish ministers to join me in regular meetings to consider policy, to be informed about major decisions and to keep me advised as to what was happening in their departments. I had two undersecretaries, two law officers and a Scottish whip and my PPS also attended. Law officers are usually kept in their law place but there is too great a tendency for colleagues once they enter a government to become involved in the rivalries among their offices and only to see and speak to each other at formal meetings. At the Ministry of Aircraft Production, I had evidently created a sensation by actually ringing up the Prime Minister and speaking to him on the 'phone. It is, as I learned, the habit of ministries to conduct nearly all the business between ministers through their secretaries and certainly, a junior minister through his chief. On the other hand, I was probably too prone to get ahead and do the job without keeping everyone informed. Indeed, it was an instruction of mine that none of the Scottish ministers was to seek kudos for what we were doing but to let our actions speak for themselves. A good deal had been done before I took office. Tom Johnston, who was always creative and fertile in conception, had carried through the hydro-electric scheme and was now its chairman. He had done much on the Forestry Commission to stimulate enterprise there. A Scottish Tourist Board had been established and under his guidance, there was a great drive to bring income to Scotland from this source.

Joe Westwood had become Secretary of State in the difficult period of emergence from the war and rehabilitation. Before the war, in Scotland there had been 140,000 building trade operatives of whom 60,000 were skilled men. At the end of the war these numbers were reduced to 40,000 operatives of whom 25,000 were skilled. Shortages of material required a continuation of licensing and controls and, in the first task of building houses, there was frustration after frustration.

The leader of the Scottish building trade at a later period, in answer to my question why they were not completing more houses, replied that it was because too many houses had been ordered. This may seem a paradox but it was exactly the situation I was faced with when I took office. George Buchanan, it is said, was offered the Ministry of Pensions but asked Mr Attlee to send him to Scotland to get on with the houses. Under Joe Westwood he was given this responsibility and he certainly put drive into the job. It suffered, however, from the defects of Lord Beaverbrook's drive for aircraft. He made an appeal for everyone capable to get into the aircraft industry and men left garages and all kinds of occupations and flocked to aircraft works and upset great areas of production.

But, of course, production just does not work that way. In the building of houses, the same rules must be followed that are needed for the production of motor cars, tanks, and even the most highly mass-produced articles, such as typewriters. Success and efficiency depend upon components reaching the required place in exactly the right proportion without fail, so that at no point is the progress from start to finish held up. There was little possibility, of course, of any such scientific organisation of the production of houses without long delays at the start, so George Buchanan placed the orders and drove everyone to get on with the job with the result that when I came on the scene we had thousands of houses under construction but few ready for occupation. They were held up for different reasons. At most places, it was shortage of timber. Then it was, in turn, baths, taps, electric fittings, iron water and drain pipes, especially the bends, glass and even water. Some contractors were going out and buying electric fittings in Woolworth's to finish off their uncompleted houses.

Perhaps the case of glass illustrates the point best. After the war, there was no shortage of milk. Liquid milk, because of rationing, and the children's milk was being consumed in quantities far greater than pre-war. The need for delivery bottles alone was engaging much of the capacity of the glass works. The demand ran into millions of bottles. In addition, there was the demand for windows for houses at an unprecedented rate. We therefore ran into shortages and houses were standing almost finished waiting for windows. I started on this problem. We found that the bottle neck was the lack of soda ash which came from factories, I think at Cheshire. To increase the supply, a new factory was needed but this was going to demand the expenditure of some millions of pounds and a delay of some years to develop. There was therefore no sense in pushing the builders beyond the materials available.

I had therefore the unpleasant task of issuing instructions to stop starting new houses and turn the available joinery and plumbing labour on to finishing some of the houses waiting for completion. This step very soon resulted in an increase of the houses becoming ready for occupation. The Scottish building industry before the war was organised to produce 20,000 houses, according to a report in the *Edinburgh Evening News* for May 1934. Mr G.W. Clark[3] who read the report said the English worker expected a house of four rooms, one of which was not used as a bedroom, whereas the Scottish worker had had to be content with two rooms and in some cases one. A commission which had sat during the war in its report laid down new standards for Scottish housing. 50,000 houses a year were needed for ten years to make up the leeway and provide houses of the new standard required. There was no way in which a building industry equipped to build 20,000 pre-war houses with the production and delivery of materials geared to pre-war numbers could possibly reach the targets demanded after the war. Especially as the pre-war industry personnel were not there.

I refused to be part of the political nonsense that the number of houses built could be either credited to or blamed on the government of the day. I gave instructions that none of the ministers or civil servants were to boast of achievements or to prophesy about miracles to come. Moreover, I stated publicly that I did not consider houses to be the first priority. It was more important that Scotland should earn its living and factories came first. One of my under-secretaries found it difficult to restrain himself and embarrassed us on several occasions by making too optimistic estimates of what was going to happen. John Robertson[4] had been given responsibility for housing but already he was suffering in health and finding it difficult to apply his mind to grasping all the ramifications of this complex problem and, as it was public dynamite as a political issue, I had to add the day to day questions of housing to

---

[3]   Gilbert Wildridge Clark, author of a classic social survey *The Housing of the Working Classes of Scotland* (Glasgow: H. Nisbet & Co., 1930).

[4]   John Robertson (1898–1955), politician, Labour MP for Berwickshire and Haddingtonshire (later Berwickshire and East Lothian) 1945–51, joint Under-secretary of State at the Scottish Office 1947–50.

my many other preoccupations. John liked the platform part of the work.

Tom Fraser,[5] on the other hand, was almost a back-room boy in the sense that he did not bother much about making speeches but was a splendid worker. He had the responsibility mainly for agriculture and had built up a great knowledge of the subject and obtained the confidence of the farmers because he was so well informed. He was and is a hefty debater, armed both with the facts and the spirit, and he could be confidently entrusted with any debate in which he was interested. The House during this period was just a little unfair to these junior ministers. The theory was that they should take turns at answering questions – as they did under later administrations – but if I absented myself to this end, the house immediately set up a hulabaloo asking where was the Secretary of State. John Robertson did not have the quickness of mind to deal with supplementaries – he liked, quite rightly, to take time to think out his answers. But that is of no avail at question time and I saw after one or two experiences and on the advice of Stafford Cripps who had been listening in, that it was unwise to expose John to this danger for, of course, it is at the dispatch box that ministers frequently bring disaster on themselves. Dai Grenfell,[6] who was a fine Minister of Mines, used to give such long and detailed answers that every one of them opened up about another hundred supplementaries and he could not therefore cope with the overflow. It was thought that this was one of the reasons for his departure from office. I therefore wanted to protect John, though he never knew this nor would he have appreciated it.

I had two other first class colleagues in John Wheatley[7] and Douglas Johnston,[8] the Lord Advocate and Solicitor General. John Wheatley was as keen on his politics as on his law which is an exception for legal MPs. We were very well served by our legal colleagues. They were all outstanding at the bar. Lord Jowitt[9] was Lord Chancellor;

---

5   Thomas Fraser (1911–88), politician, Labour MP for Hamilton 1943–67, joint Under-secretary of State at the Scottish Office 1945–51, Minister of Transport 1964–5.
6   David Grenfell (1881–1968), politician, Labour MP for Gower 1922–59, Secretary of State for mines 1940–2, father of the House of Commons 1952–9.
7   John Thomas Wheatley, Baron Wheatley (1908–88), politician and judge, Labour MP for Edinburgh East 1947–54, Solicitor-general for Scotland 1947, Lord Advocate 1947–51.
8   Douglas Johnston, Lord Johnston (1907–85), politician and judge, Labour MP for Paisley 1948–61, Solicitor-general for Scotland 1947–51.
9   William Allen Jowitt, Earl Jowitt (1885–1957), politician and judge, Liberal MP for The Hartlepools 1922–4, Preston 1929, Labour MP for Preston 1929–31, Ashton-under-Lyne 1939–45, Attorney-general 1929–32, Solicitor-general 1940–2, Minister of National Insurance 1944–5, Lord Chancellor 1945–51.

Stafford Cripps, though Chancellor of the Exchequer, was in the Cabinet; Hartley Shawcross[10] and Frank Soskice[11] were both first class in different ways. Hartley Shawcross was favoured by nature in a charming yet forceful presence, a lovely voice and a fine legal mind but he was also a great front bench politician. Yet in some difficult issues I found that for objective opinion and a clear analysis John Wheatley was a better guide and Scotland kept England right on a number of matters. James Hoy was, of course, my PPS. No one ever had a better aide-de-camp. Nothing escapes his attention and he was invaluable in the relationships which must exist between a minister and MPs. He also, of course, took part in our ministerial conference.

Our job included dealing with all the legislation which came before the House at that busy period and though I did not realise it till I gave up, the call on our energy must have been very great. We had the Scottish Agricultural Charter, the Scottish Housing Act, Criminal Justice, and other major acts, all of which I had to master and be responsible for, even though I had invaluable colleagues. In addition, there were bills for white fish, herring, water supplies and drainage. Indeed, I was never at this period free from bills. I had also, of course, to share responsibility for United Kingdom bills such as the Representation of the People Bill and the National Health Service. It would no doubt have been enough for any minister to have been dealing with any one of these acts, as was the case with my opposites in England, but the Scottish aspect of all legislation has to be watched by the Scottish minister.

The relationships between Scotland and England are always, of course, a compromise. Tom Johnston in his day and I in mine had difficulties because we wanted to legislate about matters which England was either not ready or unwilling at the time to deal with. Two examples come to my mind – fair tribunals to deal with letting and the case of 'buy or quit' threats to property tenants. The former was later copied by England and the latter problem had to be solved by an act of Parliament. This, it was felt by other ministers, might be embarrassing in view of the demand in England and Wales to deal with leaseholds which was under consideration by a judicial committee. It is

[10]   Hartley William Shawcross, Baron Shawcross (1902–2003), lawyer, politician and businessman, Labour MP for St Helens 1945–58, Attorney-general 1945–51 (and lead British prosecuting counsel at the Nuremburg trials), President of the Board of Trade 1951.
[11]   Frank Soskice, Baron Stow Hill (1902–79), lawyer and politician, Labour MP for Birkenhead East 1945–50, Sheffield Neepsend 1950–5, Newport 1956–66, Solicitor-general 1945–51, Attorney-general 1951, Home Secretary 1964–5, Lord Privy Seal 1965–6.

in such cases that a Secretary of State for Scotland has to be strong and effective in making his case. Occasionally matters arise which become a must for a minister if he is to remain in office. In the case of my Grand Committee proposals, after I had had a preliminary go-ahead and had consulted other Scottish parties, I could not have continued had these been rejected and indeed I so informed Herbert Morrison when he raised devils about Cabinet agreement. In the event, I got unexpected unanimity. I have seen at least one other instance where a minister had to take that line.

Normally ministers get on with their own jobs and other ministers try to be helpful. Where their activities cross each other then, of course, there must be discussions among the civil servants first, and failing agreement, then among ministers. Coalitions fail usually because the failure to agree results in stagnation and no action at all. Occasionally this can happen within any government. It is especially the weakness of coalitions.

On the creative side, apart from the major legislation which we were passing in common with our southern neighbours, I had then to think out what could be done for Scotland. It is not easy for a Secretary of State to make dramatic changes. In education, for example, it would be quite improper for governments to keep changing backwards and forwards the policies on the education of children to fit in with their respective political philosophies. This, however, makes it very difficult for a government to stimulate progress against the normal inertia of a great self-confident institution. Tom Johnston used to say to me – they know we will only be here for a short time and they do not want to start up new schemes which the next minister will change. My economic conference is an example of this problem. All the trouble we went to – and the civil servants went to – to make this work came eventually to naught. Nevertheless, I lent what support I could to progress. I appreciated that there was some sense in resistance to change unless this was to be permanent. The great instrument we had were advisory committees composed of public men of high standing. There were excellent reports on primary and secondary education and these were recommended to the teaching profession.

The Secretary of State must, of course, accept responsibility and this makes it necessary for him sometimes to deviate from the recommendations. For example, one report advocated the abolition of home lessons. I thought this was too negative an approach and therefore recommended that the form of home lessons should be changed to giving the children projects which would require them to be adventurous and thus guide their out of school activities into healthy and instructive channels. It was very sad that conditions did not permit me to do more to extend nursery schools. The value of these schools is not fully recognised but a close acquaintanceship with them soon confirms that the first formative years are probably those that leave the deepest impressions. Margaret McMillan,[12] Madame Montessori[13] and others brought to these schools the combination of doing and learning. Many people confuse them with day nurseries which were established to care for children while mothers were working.

On one occasion, when I took Hector McNeil to see what had been done in Edinburgh which has an honoured place in their development, he was much impressed by what he saw. I learned there was difficulty in getting assistants. I asked the teacher in charge whether adolescent girls would be of any use. It seemed to me that this would be a fruitful activity for girls leaving school between the end of their examinations and the leaving date. They would help in the school, they would learn how to deal with children when they came to be mothers themselves and they would appreciate the value of the nursery school in education. Mothers at all times get quite a lot of education from their children attending these schools. I mentioned the matter to my wife who was on the education authority which at once accepted the idea and included it in their curriculum for mothercraft. Progress is really far less in dramatic revolutionary changes than in the multitude of little changes which taken together change our whole lives. As Marx pointed out, it is usually the need to adapt our institutions to suit the result of these changes that sometimes brings the more noticeable and sometimes violent upheavals. The developing chicken has to crack the egg to grow further.

The final stages of the negotiations of the National Health Service were concluded during my early months and along with Nye Bevan, I had to take part in the final meetings with the doctors. These negotiations had been going on since war time when Tom Johnston and the then Minister of Health in England – Mr Willink[14] – found it difficult to bring the doctors to any kind of agreed settlement. Tom during this period invited me to be present in his discussion with his advisors so I really was in on this question even before Nye Bevan. One of the difficulties was that they never put forward any real objections which had sense in them till the last meeting, when the one they did

[12] Margaret McMillan (1860–1931), socialist propagandist and educationist, promi-
      nent ILP supporter and advocate of progressive nursery education through the
      open-air Deptford 'Camp School' established in 1911.
[13] Maria Tecla Artemesia Montessori (1870–1952), Italian physician and educationist.
[14] Sir Henry Urmston Willink (1894–1973), politician and administrator, Conserva-
      tive MP for Croydon North 1940–8, Minister of Health 1943–5.

advance and which was agreed to turned out to have been a complete miscalculation of the results of the scheme.

One of their points I was able to dispose of and we never heard much more about it. The doctors insisted that in the case of dismissal for bad doctoring practice, the dismissed man must have an appeal to the courts of law. The importance of this point as an obstruction to the introduction of the National Health Service can be judged from the fact that under the old scheme, the incidence of dismissals was one doctor every thirteen years! I said this seemed a curious demand for doctors to make. It was one of the cardinal features of justice in this country that a man should be tried by his peers. Doctors who had a dispute on a point of law could appeal to the courts as seemed sensible. But how doctors could agree to a lawyer, even on the bench, deciding whether a man was a good doctor or not was beyond me. The point had never struck them and we heard no more about it.

Doctor Charles Hill[15] was the leader of the delegation or at least its chief officer, and often, of course, there was an enjoyable battle of wits between him and Nye Bevan. If Nye Bevan had any fault at all during my presence at these meetings it was his impatience in listening to irrelevant and foolish argument. He usually exasperated the doctors by answering their points before they had even time to make them. During all this I was in the unfortunate position that we in Scotland were being held up by what appeared to be the commercialism of the English doctor system. The medical profession in Scotland were ready to be reasonable and get on with the practical preparations. They had, of course, to stand alongside their BMA English colleagues but we in Scotland were far in advance of England in readiness when the scheme was launched.

On the eve of the scheme I was threatened with a strike of chemists. A delegation from the Scottish chemists came to the House of Commons to ask for guarantees of increased fees. I pointed out to them that when the scheme started, they were entitled to put in a claim which would be considered, and if agreement could not be reached they were further entitled to proceed under the Whitley Council scheme to arbitration. We could not agree and they left determined not to work the scheme which was to start the following week. Although they did not know it, their position was weakened by the fact that two great organisations were ready to work the scheme and the patients

---

[15] Dr Charles Hill, Baron Hill of Luton (1904–89), doctor, politician and broadcaster, National Liberal and Conservative MP for Luton 1950–63, Secretary of the British Medical Association 1944–50, Postmaster-general 1955–7, Chancellor of the Duchy of Lancaster 1957–61, Minister of Housing and Local Government and Welsh Affairs, 1961–2, Chairman of the BBC 1967–72.

would not have suffered. I was told later that one of their number was advised by a relative, who was a distinguished statesman on the other side of the House – Sir John Anderson, that my attitude was the proper one and that the chemists had taken up an unjustifiable attitude.

About seven o'clock that evening they came back and asked James Hoy, my PPS, for another interview. He said there was no point in this as I was busy on the front bench and could not leave the House for further argument. They assured him they had changed their view. Mr Linstead,[16] a MP who was associated with them, came along and encouraged them to be reasonable. They wanted some guarantees about the condition I had stated – that they could appeal to arbitration through the Whitley Council – and they wanted it in writing. There were no typists available at that time of night and we had to have such a pledge in duplicate. I solved the dilemma by getting an old typewriter out of my cupboard which I had used as a PPS for my correspondence, and myself typed out the agreement we had come to about their starting the scheme. The *Daily Express* got hold of the story and printed a heading which bore considerable resemblance to the irregularities of the lines and the wobbly nature of the type. This document evidently created quite a stir at a later date when they demanded its implications, though their rights as stated could hardly be denied to them as I simply stated the position as it was under the scheme. Incidentally, the Scottish chemists got 1/3d per prescription in Scotland while in England the chemists got only 9d. I suggested they might be wise not to press for an enquiry as the question might arise as to why Scotland got sixty-six per cent more than England.

It was not easy in the midst of these large and disturbing questions to get time to think about the long-term problems of Scotland. Yet in the period after the war, we were all anxious to ensure a great future for our land. The problems as I saw them were, first, to ensure that Scotland was equipped to earn a good living among the other nations of the world; secondly, as a corollary to stop its depopulation by the drift south of both industry and people; and thirdly, to provide conditions under which Scots would be able to make their own special contribution to civilisation.

On this last point, I had long been convinced that we must resist cultural uniformity and that one of the advantages of liberty was that we could think differently and give a colourful variety to life. On the other hand, economically there had to be the greatest spread of

[16] Sir Hugh Linstead (1901–87), pharmaceutical chemist and politician, Conservative MP for Wandsworth Putney 1942–64, Secretary and Registrar of the Pharmaceutical Society.

knowledge and we must not hesitate to assimilate any knowledge which could help us.

Our handicaps in the economic struggle for a good living were that we had no known raw materials other than coal, that our soil both above and below ground was less easily exploited than more favourable areas. I had to accept as a fact what many of those who made Scottish nationalist demands on the government seemed to ignore, that industry was a matter for private enterprise and not a matter under any government control or direction. Tom Johnston had already brought two organisations together as the Scottish Council (Development and Industry) first under the chairmanship of Sir William Y. Darling and then under Lord Bilsland.[17] I was careful to ensure and to assure Lord Bilsland that my proposed Economic Conference in no way intruded upon the functions of his Council and I should like to pay tribute to him for the way he resisted pressure to resign and embarrass the government. He, like myself in this matter, was more concerned with Scotland's future than with political advantage.

My power was limited to encourage the Scottish Council in work attracting new industry and the government through the Board of Trade gave it material and financial help through the industrial estates. Before I left office, factories had been built with government assistance in formerly distressed areas capable of providing jobs for 120,000 workers. These were light industries in the main and offered an insurance against slumps such as we had suffered before the war. They also had the effect of introducing new manners and brighter conditions into industry which in due course spread their influence into the older heavier industries. I tried to get everyone to realise that we could not wait for someone from the south to do things for us, we should help ourselves. Local authorities should themselves get busy to attract industries to suit their areas for if it were done on a national basis, there were 625 constituencies all making the same demands and no government could please them all. The Scottish Council have continued their good work.

Although Tom Fraser did the greater part of the ministerial work on agriculture, I took a great interest in it especially in regard to research and development. That was particularly so in regard to the second of Scotland's problems – the Highlands. Two possible extremes of policy are available. The process of depopulation can be allowed to go on unchecked which means that population will gradually withdraw from

---

[17]   Alexander Stephen Bilsland, Baron Bilsland (1892–1970), banker and business-man, Chairman of the Executive Committee of Scottish Council (Development and Industry) 1946–55.

the more inaccessible parts and large sections go back to the wild. A few people will continue, no doubt, to live there who prefer a fishing and hunting life on a low standard of [living] to a disciplined existence with modern amenities. Or, the nation must take steps to providing such amenities as are necessary to make a relatively contented habitation possible. I decided that we must start from the second premise.

This area had been the breeding ground of a people who had contributed much to the opening up and development of the world and was still the nursery of many fine men and women. Moreover, it was an area worth living in apart from its poverty of economic resources. I therefore got down to discover what was possible. In the past there had been a large number of ambulance projects, a pier here and a harbour there, but in some cases the money spent had been wasted so far as contributing to any solution was concerned. The Chancellor of the Exchequer Stafford Cripps agreed with me that in spite of the cuts necessary for the emergency of 1947, an exception would be made of a comprehensive development plan for the Highlands.

I at once set going a departmental enquiry with all the expert advice available to discover what could be done, say in a five years' period. I contacted carpet manufacturers to see whether a domestic industry was possible to complement the tourist trade in the summer and this was practicable because it used local wool. The committee reported just after I left office and my successor Hector McNeil took the plan a stage further. I persuaded my colleagues to allow a great area outside Inverness to be designated a Development Area so that it might benefit from the government assistance available to industry starting up there, and the Scottish Council then took over to try and find firms willing to start up there. With the exception of David Rollo[18] and a few other small concerns, even that help did not induce or make possible the development of industry there.

The one great hope was forestry. We prepared a fifty-year plan of afforestation to create about two and a half million acres of timber. The value of tree planting is that it brings not only work for the existing population but as the trees grow, in twenty years' time they also provide additional work for the families of the foresters. When the trees left the Highlands so did the people; as they return, population again will increase. They have the further advantage that they provide the number of people necessary to make possible the social life without which we were losing the shepherds and their families as well. As Secretary of

---

[18]   The likely reference here is to Rollo Industries, founded by John M. Rollo (1901–85), which manufactured tools at its Barrmor works near Oban. These were visited by Tom Fraser in 1948, *Scotsman*, 25 August 1948.

State responsible in Scotland for both agriculture and afforestation, it was possible to get a coordinated policy. Land could be transferred from agriculture to forestry only by the specific written authority of the Secretary of State himself. We therefore set about getting the two to work to their mutual advantage. In the Sutherland hills, where the steepness gives a quick run off to rainfall, it is difficult to get the benefit of fertilisers which are washed away. By the planting of trees along the hillside, several desirable objectives were achieved. First, the speed of drainage was slowed up by the loss due to evaporation through the trees and the barriers of their root systems. 'Gates' through the trees made it possible to keep the sheep up above the tree line for summer grazing and allow them to come down in the winter to the more sheltered and now fertile lower slopes. The production of more winter feed increased the possibility of increasing cattle which in their turn helped to destroy the bracken.

One large area in Sutherlandshire was made the subject of the first experiment. There was great difficulty in getting the cooperation of some of the owners and we were loth to use compulsory powers when so much depended on goodwill. But already in my own time, there were great improvements and every indication that such schemes would work. I saw the valley of Strathnaver filled with thriving farms which was the result of the land settlement schemes about thirty years before, and there is no doubt that that consistent and determined policy could change the face of the Highlands. But one Secretary of State's tenure of office can only plant seeds – the fruits may not appear for many years. It was some little satisfaction to read in the *Inverness Courier*, whose editor Mr Barron[19] was an independent and patriotic highlander, its summing up:

> Like Mr Woodburn – and unlike his critics – they (in the County and Town Council of Inverness) realise that the neglect of the past fifty years cannot be remedied in a brief year or two … In the Highlands today, even among those who like ourselves are not socialists, there is a feeling that at long last a genuine and sustained effort it being made to deal with the Highland problem in all its adversities and complexities and for that reason the Highland people who have never lacked faith in themselves look on the future with confidence.

---

[19] Dr Evan Macleod Barron (1880–1965), newspaper proprietor and editor and historian, took over the *Inverness Courier* from his father in 1919.

That was all a Secretary of State could achieve – to inspire people to help themselves and give what assistance the state could provide. There was at least the satisfaction also that the drift from the Highlands was halted and if the developments continue, it should be reversed in the course of time.

It has proved nearly impossible to get firms to start up. Private enterprise cannot be expected to make such sacrifices for patriotic reasons and I am now convinced that this must be done by the state. I proposed three methods. First, that private enterprise be invited to set up specific industries with specific help for the early period; failing success in that, then public authorities like the Forestry Commission, the Hydro-electric Board and the Atomic Energy Commission be asked, and failing success there, the state itself should create enterprise. I started myself with the Forestry Commission and we agreed that we might use the village of Cannich for the beginnings of a wood and furniture industry. Just before I left office, the owner of Glen Affric felt himself obliged to sell off the timber. This was going to be an amenity tragedy and I arranged for the Forestry Commission to use its powers to take over the forest. With the other woods, this made an enormous area of timber and there seemed no reason why some of it should not leave the district as finished furniture rather than as raw timber. Lord Robinson,[20] then Chairman of the Forestry Commission, was ready and Stafford Cripps agreed, but the election came just then and I am afraid the scheme fell through.

We gave a grant of £20,000,000 to help rural water and drainage developments and in the case of the Highlands with new equalisation grants – by which the State bolstered the rate income of poor areas – this meant a great deal more – probably more than ninety per cent of the cost. The total expenditure covered with local authority contributions was about £60,000,000. (England and Wales got only £15,000,000!) This equalisation grant met approximately seventy-five per cent of Local Authority Expenditure. Fishing and farming also benefited from improvement grants, housing grants and in many other ways. A great impetus was therefore given to a long-term solution of Highland problems and immediate stimulation to enterprise for the present generation.

The other basic industry of Scotland was coal. While there were up to date concerns like the Fife Coal Company and the Ayrshire Collieries, great parts of Scotland's coal field were becoming exhausted and the

[20]   Roy Lister Robinson, Baron Robinson (1883–1952), forester, Secretary to the Forestry Reconstruction (Acland) Committee in 1916 and instrumental in building up the Forestry Commission from 1919, Chairman 1932–52, Director-general 1945–7.

multitude of owners made it impossible to get any comprehensive planning for future prosperity. Nationalisation – and this was its object – made this possible. The job was really to create a new coal industry by sinking shafts to deeper seams and shifting a mining population from the exhausted mines to areas with new industry. Because it was an enterprise of the nation, the whole procedure was planned as a combined operation. A new town was created at Glenrothes and other units in Midlothian at Newbattle and Penicuik, in Ayrshire near Cumnock, and the offer of new homes made it possible to get new and young families to move into these new areas. At Tullibody in Clackmannanshire a new population of nearly 1,000 occupy entirely new houses and will develop a large new mine nearby. Mines like aeroplanes and other new machines do not come into being overnight. These new mines were going down to depths below the existing mines and, of course, were bound to meet snags not foreseen. A period of seven to eight years has to be anticipated as the time likely before they will be working full out. So the only dramatic change was in the decision – the accomplishment required time and patience.

My own participation in the atomic energy decisions was very minor as the whole procedure was subject to careful security precautions. But I was at conference on the administrative side with many of the scientists. We nearly had the Sellafield project in Scotland when it was anticipated that they would need large supplies of water. Joe Westwood was in office when the project was contemplated. He was a little doubtful of its value to us. It was clear to me then that Dr Cockcroft[21] and his colleagues, at first handicapped by America's decision to shut down the exchange of information, had actually benefited by having to think it out anew. They made a jump which took us ahead of the United States and eventually enabled us to be the first nation to produce electricity on a commercial scale from uranium. Getting things done in government is always more or less of a struggle where insistence and patience are required in equal measure. The one which gave me most personal satisfaction was not one which attracted any public interest at all.

It arose out of our first health debate on the Scottish Grand Committee. Before such a debate the minister has to get a complete review of the department's work, the state of Scotland's health and study all the subjects likely to arise in debate. On this occasion in the preliminary discussions it appeared for the first time that tuberculosis in Scotland was increasing at an alarming rate. This was the more serious because in other countries the rate of mortality was going

---

[21] Sir John Douglas Cockcroft (1897–1967), physicist and engineer, Director of the atomic energy research establishment at Harwell from 1946.

down. No one could tell me why and I had to go into the debate without any satisfactory explanation. Various suggestions were offered. Bad housing was an obvious possible one. Bad food, overtime and the effects of the war were also likely causes. Walter Elliot in the debate actually suggested it was because we had so many Polish troops here from a country with a high rate. It was possible that a new variety had been imported. It all seemed very unscientific. As Secretary of State I had a scientific advisory committee and this seemed a job they should tackle. I therefore asked them to investigate this problem. A year later, when the next debate took place, we were not much further on.

The immediate steps we had taken in 1948 when the rise was discovered was to try and stop infection from contacts. We were about to stop the production of aluminium houses. We ordered another 1,000 which were allocated to those authorities who were prepared to allocate houses to TB contacts so that this barrier to infection could be established at once. No doubt this helped. But after a year all that we got from the investigation was to discover that the increase was confined to two sections – young women between sixteen and twenty-five and old men over fifty-three. All the other groups were having a lower death rate. I felt that the whole range of medical research was unsatisfactory in as much as we had no authority whose business it was to organise such research.

I proposed therefore to set up, in conjunction with my scientific advisory committee, a medical research organisation. I pointed out that in the existing set up I had an institute for the study of the diseases of the potato and another for the study of diseases of animals and their nutrition. There was no such organisation for human beings. The Medical Research Council was asked to comment and I had a memo from its chairman saying that it was not practical to organise medical research. It was when someone was inspired to undertake such investigations that they gave grants and assistance. I noted on the memo that this theory was nonsense for both insulin and penicillin had been the result of organised research. Then Sir Edward Mellanby[22] came along to see me and I had to convince him. His case collapsed when he told me that a wealthy Scot had given Edinburgh Royal Infirmary £4,000 to stimulate research on heart troubles. I asked how it was possible for this public-spirited gentleman to organise research and the government could not? He then said that to his knowledge such a conversation as ours had never taken place with a minister before. However, he agreed.

---

[22] Sir Edward Mellanby (1884–1955), medical scientist and administrator, Secretary of the Medical Research Council 1933–49.

So we proceeded to invite the heads of the Scottish medical schools and of the universities along with my scientific advisory committee, with Sir Andrew Davidson,[23] Chief Medical Officer from my Office, and Sir Edward Mellanby from the Medical Research Council. I made my proposal. That we in Scotland should have an organisation for the stimulation guidance and control of research in medicine and that this should cover all the three bodies represented. It would run in harmony with the Medical Research Council. The lines of development which struck me as being useful were first of all to find out what research was being done in Scotland, what facilities in Scotland existed and whether there were individuals capable of doing such research who could be allocated to specific problems. I was met, to my surprise, with a reiteration of this theory that medical research was not susceptible to organisation. I said I seemed to have heard of the Mayo Institute in the United States and other institutions such as Brantings.

We then got agreement and the way was set to begin the work. Later some difficulties arose with the Medical Research Council. I think Sir Edward Mellanby was apprehensive lest this new organisation cut across the authority of the MRC but the patience and wise negotiations of Sir Andrew Davidson with Sir Edwards's successor finally brought consent and Scotland got its own organisation for research. More than that, I recommended them to apply to the Hospital Endowments Commission for funds and in due course Parliament passed an act setting up a fund which guarantees to Scottish research the necessary funds.

I was convinced that Scotland could not remain a first-class school of medicine on second-hand research and that it must have the means of making its own contribution. It is not often that a minister sees any pet scheme actually coming to realisation in his own term of office. I felt that from the small beginnings of this organisation, Scotland would yet draw strength to add still further to one of its great contributions to civilisation in its doctors and nurses.

At the Election in 1950 the Labour Party had good progress to report both in actual achievement and in laying foundations for the future. Not long before the election, MP Niall McPherson[24] had raised a debate on home rule and as chance would have it, the previous debate finished early and Scotland had nearly the whole day for the subject. Normally the Under-secretary replies to adjournment debates

---

[23] Sir Andrew Davidson (1892–1962), doctor and administrator, Chief Medical Officer of the Department of Health for Scotland 1941–54.
[24] Niall Macpherson, Baron Drumalbyn (1908–87), politician, National Liberal and Conservative MP for Dumfriesshire 1945–63, Minister of Pensions and National Insurance 1962–3.

but as this debate was broadened out, both John Wheatley and I spoke. I quoted from the *Edinburgh Evening News and Dispatch* and from John – now Lord Cameron[25] – some comments which made clear that few people holding responsibility in the life of Scotland supported home rule. At that time the Zionists were sending bombs in packets to public persons and I reproached Dr John MacCormick[26] for having lightly said nothing would be done for Scotland till a bomb was sent to 10 Downing Street. In view of the fact that some foolish Scottish nationalists had actually thrown bombs in Glasgow it seemed to me the suggestion might have been followed by the more fanatical section as I had information that other preparations for violence were in train. This suggestion of bombs created great headlines and the press poured ridicule on my head, though later my warnings were fully justified.

I mention this because when I ceased to be Secretary of State in 1951 it was generally assumed by the Scottish nationalists that I had been penalised for my attitude to them. Far from that having influenced either the election or my position, the Labour government of 1951 was only rendered possible because we in Scotland did not lose one seat. No one, of course, except a Prime Minister knows all the reasons for his choice of ministers. There are things which are well known. First, it is the custom, sometimes quite irrational I think, to switch ministers round. It is supposed to freshen ministers up and give hope to potential ministers. Ministers can become stale. One change may involve many. Junior ministers may have qualified for promotion and their minister will advance their claims. These can be satisfied only if vacancies occur in the senior ranks.

In my case, the Prime Minister said they wanted me to remain in the government and they'd like me to take over Fuel and Power. William Whiteley,[27] who was a miner and the Chief Whip and with Ernest Bevin was among the closest confidants of the Prime Minister, I gather, thought I was the man for Fuel and Power. From a personal political point of view, it would have been a return to a United Kingdom ministry and to British politics – the Secretary of State for Scotland is almost confined to his own Scottish MPs – and as a ministry it had interesting possibilities. The Prime Minister evidently thought it was

[25] Sir John Cameron, Lord Cameron (1900–96), judge.
[26] John MacDonald MacCormick (1904–61), politician and Scottish nationalist, founder of Glasgow University Scottish Nationalist Association 1927 and prominent within the National Party of Scotland 1928–32 and the Scottish National Party 1932–42. Thereafter he was an instrumental figure in the establishment of the Scottish Convention in 1947 and the Scottish Covenant Association.
[27] William Whiteley (1881–1955), politician and trade unionist, Labour MP for Blaydon 1922–31, 1935–55, chief whip 1942–55.

a good thing. I, however, took the view that the change would be misinterpreted because of the campaign of the Scottish nationalists – of which, incidentally, he was almost unaware – and that it would be a wasteful interruption of the plans afoot. I also thought that others could do Fuel and Power as well as I and I saw no reason to pull up my Scottish roots unless I was really needed elsewhere. Hector McNeil was already advised and I decided to decline the invitation.

The Prime Minister asked me to take some time to think it over which I did but finally I begged leave to decline and I once more became a back-bencher. Hector told me he did not want to be Secretary of State. Others said Ernest Bevin wanted him to be promoted and no doubt the Secretaryship of Scotland was a suitable Ministry. The exchange seemed satisfactory and I felt considerable regret at feeling compelled to resign. I had always recognised that it would be difficult to leave the Secretaryship of Scotland for any other normal ministry and in the event, I found it impossible. One of the Sunday press visited me to find out what job I was going to. His editor had said it could not be less than a £10,000 a year job when I left Downing Street with such a smile.

CHAPTER TEN

I did not know I had been working so hard till I was out of office but the change involved a considerable amount of readjustment. We were still the government and this made it difficult for me to be active in the House. To have become a critic of the government would have been open to misinterpretation as would also an overzealous support. I therefore vegetated for a while. There were many activities outside the public sphere where interesting work could be done and ex-ministers are called upon to do jobs for which ministers are not available.

One such was being asked by the Interparliamentary Association to lead the first delegation of MPs to the new German parliament. By pure chance I found myself paying three visits to Germany in 1951. The first was on my own account. I went to visit a trade union educational school at Dortmund and my wife and I continued up the Rhine on to Innsbruck, visiting places of interest on the way. I was able to speak to the German 'man in the street' and get his point of view. After I returned I was asked to go with a delegation of three MPs to lecture at German universities and colleges at Hanover, Göttingen, Aachen and Dusseldorf to explain the respective Labour, Tory and Liberal policies but also with a view to showing them how our democracy worked, especially that three people of different political parties could debate their points of view without being personal antagonists.

In the meantime, I had been asked to lead the first British delegation of MPs to Bonn, Wiesbaden and Berlin. I had in this way an unique opportunity of discussing the German problem in the space of a few months with all sections from the President himself to the car conductor. The chief interest was of course the visit to the Bonn parliament. The evening before, Dr Ehlers,[1] who was the 'speaker' of the Bundestag, asked me closely about our question time and on the House of Commons, then suggested that I might in my address

[1]   Hermann Ehlers (1904–54), West German politician, president of the Bundestag 1950–4.

tell something about our practice. It was also suggested that I speak partly in German and partly in English. The MPs would, they said, be delighted to think we spoke their language and yet also they wanted to feel that they could understand when we spoke in our own. I had therefore the very great honour of being the first foreigner to address the German Bundestag. In the evening, when he entertained us to dinner, Mr Adenauer,[2] the Chancellor, who had heard about the address, wanted me to tell him all about question time but though he expressed his admiration of the idea he thought it would not work in Germany. But Dr Ehlers was right – the Bundestag did create a question time and it worked.

Thereafter we visited Wiesbaden, Frankfurt, Berlin and Hamburg to pay our respects to the Land Government of these areas and we attended a session of the Berlin Parliament when Dr Reuter[3] issued his challenge to the East German government to allow the freely elected representatives of that section of Berlin to take their places which were being held empty for them.

By this time we had been advised of the impending general election in Britain and had to make our way home. That election ended for the time being the period of the most eventful Parliament of all time where the class struggle division of Britain into the 'two nations' of Disraeli gave way to the greatest peaceful social revolution of history to a welfare state capitalism, where no one dared argue against a just society. Governments disputed which party could govern it best.

My *Outline of Finance*, which had gone through several editions practically unchanged for fifteen years, had to be rewritten to describe the entirely new system of national finance and economic planning. Fifty years of a Labour Party influencing government and itself being the Government had carried through a peaceful social revolution with less bitterness and objection than had attended one budget of Lloyd George's in 1912.

Being in politics is an unsettling life but for me it has been a period of great creative interest and it has been a privilege to play even a small part in the great change. I am by temperament too catholic in my interests – a friend wanted me to become a doctor and I was interested in medicine; I had been interested in the law, both very natural to a Scot, and I loved practical things. But political life has made it possible for me to interest myself in all of these at least from the outside. Winston Churchill was once asked if he was a supporter of the church.

---

[2]   Konrad Hermann Joseph Adenauer (1876–1967), West German politician, chancellor of the Federal Republic of Germany 1949–63.

[3]   Ernst Rudolf Johannes Reuter (1889–1953), West German politician, governing mayor of West Berlin 1947–53.

He replied 'I can hardly describe myself as a pillar of the church – perhaps I might call myself a buttress – I support it from the outside'. I have been able to indulge many of my interests vicariously.

Members of Parliament in Britain find themselves acting regularly as hosts to visitors from nearly every country in the world. I was often kept busy with foreign MPs and delegations which were being received officially. On one occasion, when I was showing an Argentine delegation round, I pointed out the well-known personalities of Parliament as we encountered them – Mr Churchill, Mr Harold Macmillan, the then Prime Minister, Mr Hugh Gaitskell[4] the Leader of the Labour Party and so on. At that time Christopher Chataway,[5] who has later served in two Conservative administrations, had just become an MP. He had recently won world acclaim by his running the mile in less than four minutes and I was sure the delegation would be honoured and delighted to meet him. When I introduced him, I was more than pleased at their pleasure. I thought little more about it till three months later when I received a letter from the wife of the Labour attaché in Buenos Aires who had accompanied the delegation. She recalled the visit and said it had been the highlight of their stay in Britain. She said she had been surprised at the excitement the delegation displayed when they shook hands with Chris Chataway and only understood why when they all got back to their hotel. The delegation thought they had been meeting Lord Chatterley!

Of course, those MPs who speak the language of the visitors are only too willing to help and the Foreign Office invites an MP from each of the main parties to entertain them. MPs are mostly members of the Interparliamentary Union and various British American, Latin American, Franco British, British Italian, Anglo German and other associations exist. This is repeated for all the countries of the Commonwealth. Probably no country has slavishly adopted the British parliamentary system but all are interested in and acknowledge the value they have received from British experience in democracy.

---

[4] Hugh Gaitskell (1906-63), politician, Labour MP for Leeds South 1945-63, Minister for Power 1947-50, Chancellor of the Exchequer 1950-1, Leader of the Labour Party 1955-63.

[5] Christopher Chataway (1931-2014), athlete, politician and broadcaster, Conservative MP for Lewisham North 1959-66, Chichester 1969-74.

INDEX